THE INTRICACIES OF

ONLINE PRIVACY & DATA PROTECTION

AKINSOLA ABAYOMI

CONTENTS

ACKNOWLEDGMENTS

I would like to extend my heartfelt thanks to those who have been a part of this journey. Your support, encouragement, and belief in this project have meant more than words can express. To the friends and family who offered their understanding and patience, your presence has been a constant source of strength.

A special thank you to those who provided invaluable feedback and insights, helping to shape this work into what it is today. Your thoughtful contributions have been instrumental in refining and enhancing the narrative.

To everyone who believed in the vision and offered moral support, your enthusiasm and faith have been a driving force. Your kind words and positive energy have been deeply motivating.

I am profoundly grateful for the inspiration and creativity that surrounds this endeavor. This book stands as a testament to the collective effort and shared passion of those who have been part of this experience.

Thank you for walking this path with me and for making this journey both meaningful and memorable.

CHAPTER ONE

NAVIGATING ONLINE PRIVACY AND DATA PROTECTION

In this current dispensation, where every online interaction can potentially be tracked, recorded, and analyzed, safeguarding online privacy and data protection has become more crucial than ever. This chapter provides an in-depth exploration of online privacy, data protection mechanisms, and practical steps individuals and organizations can take to safeguard their information. Through real-world examples from around the globe, this chapter illustrates the principles and practices that are vital for ensuring effective data protection.

Understanding Online Privacy and Data Protection

Online privacy encompasses the right to control personal information and to ensure that such information remains confidential and secure from unauthorized access. The rapid advancement of digital technologies and the extensive use of the internet have raised significant concerns about how personal data is handled and protected.

Protecting personal data is essential for several key reasons. Firstly, it helps prevent identity theft and various forms of cybercrime, safeguarding individuals from potentially devastating financial and emotional harm. Secondly, ensuring online privacy is vital for preserving autonomy and freedom, as it allows individuals to express themselves and engage in online activities without fear of undue surveillance or exposure. For businesses, robust data protection measures are equally critical, as they build and maintain customer trust and uphold the company's reputation. In essence, effective personal security not only shields individuals from threats but also fosters a more secure and trustworthy online environment.

Data protection refers to the practices and measures implemented to safeguard personal and sensitive information from unauthorized access, misuse, disclosure, alteration, or destruction. It encompasses a range of strategies, including encryption, access controls, and secure storage, designed to ensure that data remains confidential, integral, and available only to authorized individuals. Effective data protection aims to prevent data breaches and privacy violations, thereby maintaining the trust of individuals and organizations while complying with relevant legal and regulatory requirements. Ultimately, it is about securing information against threats and ensuring its proper handling and use in a manner that respects and upholds privacy rights. There are also certain key concepts in data protection namely:

Data Collection and Consent: This involves obtaining clear, informed consent before collecting personal information. This principle is reflected in regulations like the General Data Protection Regulation (GDPR) in Europe and similar laws worldwide.

Data Minimization: It is collecting only the data necessary for a specific purpose. This principle helps mitigate risks associated with data breaches and misuse

Data Security: It encompasses measures taken to protect data from unauthorized access and breaches. This includes both technical solutions like encryption and organizational practices like regular security audits.

When ensuring the principles of online privacy and data protection are met, one must ensure that accuracy, integrity, accountability, storage limitation, confidentiality and security are reflected in each of their processes.

Real-Life Cases of Data Breaches

Examining real-life data breaches helps illustrate the importance of online privacy and the impact of inadequate data protection.

Case 1: The Singapore Health Services Data Breach (2018)

In 2018, Singapore experienced a major data breach involving the country's largest health services group, Sing Health. The breach exposed the personal and medical information of 1.5 million patients, including Prime Minister Lee Hsien Loong. The attackers exploited vulnerabilities in the network to gain unauthorized access to sensitive data. It was also linked to inadequate training of staff and slow response in fixing vulnerabilities.

Impact: The breach raised concerns about the security of personal health information and led to increased scrutiny of data protection practices within Singapore's healthcare sector.

Lessons Learned: The incident underscored the need for robust cybersecurity measures, including regular system audits and enhanced network security protocols.

Case 2: The British Airways Data Breach (2018)

In 2018, British Airways suffered a significant data breach that compromised the personal and financial details of around 380,000 customers. The breach occurred due to a vulnerability in the airline's website, which allowed attackers to intercept and steal customer data during the payment process. The attack was carried out by exploiting the account of a compromised third party to gain entry into British Airways' systems. Once inside, the attackers escalated their privileges by discovering an unsecured administrator password.

Impact: The breach resulted in substantial financial penalties and reputational damage for British Airways. It also highlighted the importance of securing online payment systems and protecting customer information.

Lessons Learned: The case demonstrated the need for rigorous testing and monitoring of online payment systems to prevent data breaches and ensure customer data protection.

Case 3: The Cambridge Analytica Scandal (2018)

The Cambridge Analytica scandal involved the unauthorized collection of personal data from millions of Facebook users for political advertising purposes. The data was harvested through a third-party app and used to influence voter behavior during elections.

Impact: The scandal led to widespread criticism of data handling practices and increased scrutiny of social media platforms. It prompted legislative changes and heightened awareness about data privacy.

Lessons Learned: The incident emphasized the importance of transparency and consent in data collection practices, as well as the need for stringent regulations governing data usage by third parties.

Case 4: Equifax Data Breach (2017)

In 2017, Equifax, one of the largest credit reporting agencies in the United States, experienced a significant data breach that exposed the personal information of approximately 147 million individuals. The breach occurred due to a vulnerability in Equifax's web application framework that had not been patched. The stolen data included sensitive information such as Social Security numbers, birth dates, and addresses.

Impact: The exposure of sensitive data significantly heightened the risk of identity theft and fraud for millions of individuals. In response to this breach, Equifax encountered severe legal and financial consequences, culminating in a substantial $700 million settlement to address consumer claims and regulatory penalties. This financial fallout underscored the serious implications of inadequate data protection and the extensive repercussions for both individuals and organizations involved.

Lessons Learned: The incident underscored the crucial need for timely patching of known vulnerabilities to prevent their exploitation. It highlighted how promptly addressing these weaknesses is essential for safeguarding systems. Additionally, organizations are now urged to adopt robust security measures and conduct regular system audits. These proactive steps are vital for identifying and mitigating potential risks, ensuring a more secure and resilient infrastructure against future threats.

These are a few examples to help us comprehend the importance of putting in place the necessary frameworks to ensure adequate security in these areas and the tremendous impact they have on individuals, businesses and communities.

There are legal frameworks guiding these concepts and providing processes to follow in ensuring privacy and data protection. Each country and region of the world have peculiarities and varying levels of implementation of these laws. It is important to understand each country's specific needs and how they have adopted laws that guide their activities in these areas. The European Union's General Data Protection Regulation (GDPR) stands as a comprehensive and influential model, setting rigorous standards for data handling, consent, and individual rights within the EU. In the United States, various sector-specific regulations like the California Consumer Privacy Act (CCPA) offer state-level protections, while federal laws such as the Health Insurance Portability and Accountability Act (HIPAA) focus on specific types of data. Other regions have their own regulations, such as Brazil's Lei Geral de Proteção de Dados (LGPD), which mirrors aspects of the GDPR, and Japan's Act on the Protection of Personal Information (APPI), which provides privacy protections in a different cultural and legal context. In Africa, data protection laws are evolving, with South Africa's Protection of Personal Information Act (POPIA) establishing significant privacy standards. Nigeria has also made strides with the Nigeria Data Protection Regulation (NDPR), which aims to enhance data protection and privacy in line with global best practices. These frameworks collectively reflect a global trend toward stricter data protection standards and emphasize the importance of privacy in an increasingly globalized world.

Best Practices for Protecting Online Privacy and Data Safety

There are various measures to be taken in safeguarding online privacy and data.

Strong Passwords and Authentication: Using strong, unique passwords for each online account is essential for preventing unauthorized access. Enabling multi-factor authentication (MFA) adds an extra layer of security by requiring additional verification. A user who employs a password manager to generate and store complex passwords and enables MFA on their accounts is better protected against unauthorized access.

Regular Software Updates: Keeping software up to date is crucial for protecting against vulnerabilities. Regular updates include patches and fixes for known security issues. This practice helps to close vulnerabilities that could be exploited by attackers to gain unauthorized access to sensitive data.

Privacy Settings and Permissions: Reviewing and adjusting privacy settings on online platforms helps control the amount of personal information shared. Regularly reviewing app permissions is also important to ensure they align with privacy preferences.

Data Encryption: Encrypting sensitive data helps ensure its confidentiality and integrity. Encryption transforms data into a format that can only be read by those with the appropriate decryption key. An organization that encrypts customer data both in transit and at rest enhances its ability to protect information from unauthorized access.

Effective and Strong Access Controls: Implementing stringent access controls ensures that only authorized individuals can access sensitive information. This involves using multi-factor authentication (MFA) to add an extra layer of security, requiring users to provide additional verification beyond just a password. By carefully managing who can access what data and under what conditions, organizations can better protect against unauthorized access and potential breaches.

Be Cautious with Personal Information and Sharing: It's important to be mindful of the personal information you share online, particularly on social media platforms. Avoid oversharing details that could be used to guess passwords or answer security questions. Regularly review and adjust the privacy settings on your social media accounts and other online platforms to control who can see your information and how it is used. By managing what you share and who has access to it, you can better protect your online privacy.

Recognize Phishing Attempts: Be careful of unsolicited emails, messages, or phone calls asking for personal information or directing you to suspicious websites. Phishing attempts often appear legitimate but aim to steal your data. Look for red flags such as misspelled URLs, generic greetings, or urgent language. Always verify the authenticity of requests by contacting the organization directly through official channels before providing any sensitive information.

Manage Your Digital Footprint: Periodically review and manage your online accounts, including deleting those you no longer use. Check the permissions and data access settings of apps and services linked to your accounts. Consider using services that let you see what data is being collected and make informed decisions about what you're comfortable sharing. This helps minimize unnecessary exposure and keeps your digital footprint under control.

Navigating online privacy and data protection requires a thorough understanding of the principles, practices, and legal frameworks that govern the digital environment. By recognizing the importance of personal privacy, adhering to data protection regulations, and implementing best practices, individuals and organizations can better safeguard their information and mitigate the risks associated with the exposure of the internet in this age. As technology continues to evolve, ongoing vigilance and adaptation are essential for maintaining robust online privacy and data protection. Staying informed about emerging threats and advancements in cybersecurity will enable individuals and organizations to navigate the complexities of online privacy with greater confidence and resilience.

CHAPTER TWO

THE ANATOMY OF A CYBERATTACK

Privacy breaches are an ever-present risk, impacting individuals, businesses, and governments alike especially as more activities are carried out online. This chapter explores the multifaceted nature of privacy breaches, detailing how they occur, the methods employed by attackers, and the systemic weaknesses that facilitate these breaches. Understanding these mechanisms is critical for developing robust defenses and strategies to protect sensitive information.

How Privacy Breaches Occur

A privacy breach occurs when unauthorized individuals gain access to personal, sensitive, or confidential information. This breach can result from various vectors, including cyberattacks, insider threats, or even human error. The impact of a privacy breach can be severe, ranging from identity theft and financial loss to reputational damage and legal consequences. There are common methods of privacy breaches employed by these malicious actors.

Phishing: Phishing is a prevalent and effective method used by attackers to deceive individuals into divulging sensitive information. Phishing attacks often involve fraudulent emails or messages that appear to be from legitimate sources, such as banks or online services. These communications typically contain malicious links or attachments designed to capture login credentials or install malware.

Social Engineering: This extends beyond phishing and encompasses a broader range of tactics aimed at manipulating individuals into revealing confidential information. This can include pretexting (where an attacker creates a fabricated scenario to obtain information) and baiting (where an attacker lures individuals with promises of rewards or information).

Malware: This is also referred to as malicious software and is designed to infiltrate and compromise systems. It includes viruses, worms, Trojans, ransomware, and spyware. Once installed on a system, malware can infiltrate data, log keystrokes, or encrypt files for random. Ransomware attacks, in particular, have surged in recent years, with attackers encrypting a victim's data and demanding payment for the decryption key.

Exploiting Vulnerabilities: Software and hardware vulnerabilities are common targets for attackers. Exploiting these vulnerabilities allows unauthorized access to systems or data. Vulnerabilities can arise from coding errors, outdated software, or configuration issues. Attackers use techniques such as buffer overflows, SQL injection, and cross-site scripting (XSS) to exploit these weaknesses.

Insider Threats: This involves individuals within an organization who misuse their access to data or systems. These threats can be malicious or inadvertent. Malicious insiders may intentionally steal or misuse information, while inadvertent insiders might accidentally expose data due to lack of awareness or training. Effective access controls and monitoring are essential to mitigate the risk of insider threats.

 Physical Theft or Loss: Physical theft or loss of devices, such as laptops, smartphones, or external drives, can lead to privacy breaches if the devices contain sensitive information. Encryption and secure storage practices are crucial in protecting data in case of physical device loss or theft.

Human Error: Human error is a significant factor in many privacy breaches. Mistakes such as sending sensitive information to the wrong recipient, misconfiguring security settings, or failing to apply software updates can expose data to unauthorized access. Continuous training and awareness programs are vital in reducing human error and reinforcing best practices.

There are emerging threats and trends in this field which cannot be overlooked. The ever-changing nature of the digital ecosystem necessitates the need to always be alert for the new and evolving forms of attacks that might be employed. One of such is Advanced Persistent Threats (APTs). These are sophisticated and long-term cyberattacks designed to infiltrate and persist within a target network. APTs typically involve multiple stages, including initial compromise, lateral movement within the network, and data exfiltration. These attacks are often carried out by well-resourced and skilled adversaries, such as nation-states or organized crime groups. Another form is called Internet of Things (IoT) Vulnerabilities. The proliferation of IoT devices introduces new vulnerabilities and attack vectors. Many IoT devices lack robust security features, making them susceptible to exploitation. Compromised IoT devices can be used to access networks, conduct distributed denial-of-service (DDoS) attacks, or exfiltrate data.

Cloud Security Concerns are among the emerging trends. As organizations increasingly adopt cloud services, ensuring the security of cloud environments becomes crucial. Misconfigured cloud settings, inadequate access controls, and vulnerabilities in cloud services can lead to data breaches. Organizations must implement comprehensive cloud security measures, including encryption, access management, and regular security assessments.

Systematic Flaws in Frameworks that Facilitate Breaches

It is imperative to highlight certain weaknesses that aid in the occurrence of privacy breaches across organizations and even in individual settings.

Inadequate Data Protection Policies: Organizations often face significant challenges due to inadequate data protection policies and insufficient data classification. When data protection policies are poorly defined or not regularly updated, there is a lack of clear guidance on handling and safeguarding sensitive information, leading to inconsistent practices and increased risk of unauthorized access and misuse. Additionally, failing to classify data effectively impedes the implementation of appropriate security measures based on the sensitivity of the information. Without proper classification, high-risk data may not receive the necessary security controls, resulting in potential mishandling and heightened vulnerability to breaches.

Weak Access Controls: Ineffective management of user access rights and failure to implement the principle of least privilege are critical weaknesses in data security. Poorly managed user access, often resulting from inadequate role-based access controls (RBAC) or outdated access reviews, can grant excessive permissions to individuals. This scenario significantly increases the risk of unauthorized access to sensitive data, whether from internal misuse or external attacks. Additionally, when organizations do not enforce the principle of least privilege, users may have access to more data than necessary for their roles. This broad access can lead to both intentional and unintentional data exposure, further compromising data security.

Outdated or Vulnerable Software: Unpatched software and obsolete systems are significant vulnerabilities in data security. Software that is not regularly updated with security patches can become a prime target for attackers, who exploit known weaknesses to gain unauthorized access or carry out malicious activities. Similarly, outdated or unsupported systems, which no longer receive security updates or vendor support, present a considerable risk. These legacy systems often lack modern security features, making them more susceptible to attacks and easier targets for those looking to exploit known vulnerabilities. Regular patching and updates, along with phasing out outdated systems, are essential to maintaining system integrity and protecting against potential threats.

Insecure Network Configurations: Weak network security and unencrypted communications are critical factors that compromise data protection. Poorly configured network security devices, such as firewalls and routers, can leave an organization's network vulnerable to unauthorized access. Inadequate network segmentation further exacerbates this risk by allowing attackers to move laterally within the network once they gain initial entry. To safeguard network infrastructure, it is essential to ensure proper configuration and segmentation. Additionally, failing to encrypt data transmitted over networks exposes sensitive information to potential interception and eavesdropping.

Techniques like man-in-the-middle attacks can easily exploit unencrypted communications, making it vital to implement strong encryption protocols for data in transit to maintain confidentiality and protect against such threats.

Human Error: Lack of training and awareness, coupled with insecure practices, significantly contributes to privacy breaches. Inadequate training and awareness programs often leave employees vulnerable to human error, such as falling victim to phishing attacks or mishandling sensitive information. Without proper education in security best practices, these errors can lead to significant data exposure. Additionally, insecure practices—such as using weak passwords, neglecting to lock devices, or improperly handling sensitive data—create vulnerabilities that can be exploited. To address these issues, organizations must implement strong security policies and ensure that employees adhere to them, while also providing ongoing training and awareness initiatives to mitigate risks and enhance overall data protection.

Inadequate Incident Response and Monitoring: Poor incident response planning and insufficient monitoring and logging are major weaknesses that can exacerbate the impact of privacy breaches. An organization lacking a well-defined incident response plan may struggle to manage breaches effectively, leading to delays in containment, remediation, and communication. This lack of structure can significantly worsen the breach's consequences. Similarly, without comprehensive monitoring and logging systems, organizations may fail to detect suspicious activities or breaches in a timely manner. Effective monitoring and detailed logging are essential for identifying potential security incidents, tracing activities, and investigating breaches to prevent future occurrences. Ensuring both robust incident response planning and thorough monitoring can greatly enhance an organization's ability to respond to and mitigate the effects of security threats.

Vendor and Third-Party Risks: Insecure third-party services and lack of due diligence pose significant risks to data security. Organizations that depend on third-party vendors for services such as cloud storage or payment processing may find that inadequate security measures from these vendors create vulnerabilities in the overall security chain. Without proper vetting and security assessments, these third-party services can become weak links, exposing sensitive data to potential breaches. Additionally, insufficient due diligence in evaluating third-party vendors can lead organizations to partner with entities that do not adhere to robust security practices. To mitigate these risks, it is crucial to conduct thorough evaluations and ensure that all third parties follow stringent security standards, thereby maintaining comprehensive data protection.

Physical Security Weaknesses: Inadequate physical access controls and poor device security are critical factors that can compromise data protection. Weak physical security measures, such as unrestricted access to facilities or improper storage of physical records, can result in unauthorized access to sensitive information. To counteract these risks, effective physical security measures, including stringent access restrictions and surveillance, are essential for preventing physical theft or loss of data. Also, unsecured devices like laptops, smartphones, or external drives pose a significant risk if they contain sensitive information. If such devices are lost or stolen and their data is not encrypted or otherwise protected, it can lead to severe data breaches. Implementing robust device encryption and secure storage practices is crucial for safeguarding sensitive information and mitigating potential risks.

Poor Data Disposal Practices: Proper data disposal practices are critical for protecting sensitive information. Insecure deletion of data, such as merely deleting files without using secure wipe methods, can result in data recovery by unauthorized individuals. Ensuring secure deletion or physical destruction of data storage media is vital to prevent unauthorized access.

Regulatory and Compliance Failures: Non-compliance with data protection regulations and inadequate documentation and auditing are significant risks to data security. Organizations that fail to adhere to regulations such as GDPR, CCPA, or HIPAA not only face legal consequences but also expose themselves to heightened vulnerability to breaches. Compliance with these regulations ensures that proper data protection measures are implemented and maintained, thereby reducing the risk of data exposure. Additionally, inadequate documentation and a lack of regular auditing can prevent the identification and mitigation of potential vulnerabilities. Without thorough documentation and frequent audits, weaknesses may go unnoticed, leading to compliance issues and an increased risk of privacy breaches. Implementing robust compliance and auditing practices is essential for maintaining effective data protection and minimizing risk.

The impact of a privacy breach extends beyond immediate data loss. Organizations may face legal repercussions, including fines and regulatory actions, particularly if they fail to comply with data protection laws such as the GDPR or CCPA. Additionally, breaches can lead to reputational damage, loss of customer trust, and financial losses due to remediation efforts and compensations. For individuals, the consequences of privacy breaches can include identity theft, financial loss, and emotional distress.

Conducting regular security assessments, including vulnerability scans, penetration tests, and risk assessments, helps identify and address potential weaknesses in systems and processes. These assessments should be part of an ongoing security strategy to ensure continuous improvement and adaptation to evolving threats.

To effectively safeguard against privacy breaches, organizations must implement a comprehensive security strategy. This includes using encryption to protect data both at rest and in transit, enforcing robust access controls to limit data access, and regularly updating software to fix vulnerabilities. Additionally, employing intrusion detection and prevention systems (IDPS) enhances the ability to identify and mitigate potential threats.

Regular security training is essential to minimize human error, covering critical topics such as phishing awareness, data handling practices, and the proper use of security tools. Furthermore, conducting ongoing security assessments, including vulnerability scans and penetration tests, is vital for identifying and addressing weaknesses in systems and processes, ensuring continuous improvement and adaptation to emerging threats.

Privacy breaches are a complex and evolving threat, driven by a variety of factors including technological vulnerabilities, human error, and sophisticated attack methods. Understanding how breaches occur is essential for developing effective strategies to protect sensitive information and mitigate the impact of such incidents.

In the following chapters, we will delve deeper and provide practical guidance on how to develop and implement robust privacy protection strategies.

CHAPTER THREE

PROTECTING DATA IN TRANSIT AND AT REST

Encryption is a cornerstone of modern cybersecurity and a critical tool for safeguarding online privacy and data. In this chapter, we delve into the mechanisms of encryption, its applications, and how it can be effectively employed to protect data both in transit and at rest. Grasping the workings of encryption is essential for anyone concerned with data security, as it provides the foundation for protecting sensitive information from unauthorized access and breaches.

The Fundamentals of Encryption

Encryption is the process of converting plain text into a coded format (cipher text) that is unreadable without the appropriate decryption key. This transformation ensures that only authorized parties can access the original data. It relies on complex algorithms and keys to encode and decode information. At its core, encryption addresses two primary concerns: confidentiality and integrity. Confidentiality ensures that data remains secret from unauthorized users. Integrity ensures that the data has not been altered or tampered with during transmission or storage. Both aspects are crucial for maintaining the security and trustworthiness of information.

There are types of encryptions, and their techniques are categorized into two main types called symmetric encryption and asymmetric encryption. In symmetric encryption, the same key is used for both encryption and decryption. This method is efficient and fast but requires secure key management to ensure that the key does not fall into the wrong hands. The Advanced Encryption Standard (AES) is a widely used symmetric encryption algorithm known for its strength and efficiency. Asymmetric encryption uses a pair of keys—one public and one private. The public key encrypts data, while the private key decrypts it. This method enhances security by not requiring the sharing of keys. RSA (Rivest-Shamir-Adleman) is a common asymmetric encryption algorithm used for secure data transmission.

Several algorithms and standards govern encryption practices. These include AES (Advanced Encryption Standard) which is a symmetric encryption standard used widely for data encryption due to its robustness and efficiency. AES supports key sizes of 128, 192, and 256 bits, with AES-256 offering the highest level of security. RSA (Rivest-Shamir-Adleman) which is an asymmetric encryption algorithm used for secure key exchange and digital signatures. RSA is known for its security but is slower compared to symmetric encryption. ECC (Elliptic Curve Cryptography) is an asymmetric encryption method that offers strong security with shorter key lengths compared to RSA. ECC is often used in mobile devices and IoT applications due to its efficiency.

Protecting Data in Transit and at Rest

Data in transit refers to information actively being transferred across networks, such as emails, file transfers, or web transactions. Protecting data in transit is crucial to prevent interception and unauthorized access. Data at rest refers to information stored on devices, servers, or cloud storage that is not actively being transferred. Protecting data at rest is essential to prevent unauthorized access and ensure data security.

These are measures to protect data in transit:

SSL/TLS Protocols: SSL (Secure Sockets Layer) and TLS (Transport Layer Security) are cryptographic protocols designed to secure data in transit over networks. TLS is the successor to SSL and provides enhanced security features.

How SSL/TLS Works:

1. Handshake Process: When a connection is established, the client and server perform a handshake to agree on encryption algorithms and exchange keys. This process ensures that both parties can securely communicate.

2. Session Encryption: Once the handshake is complete, the session data is encrypted using the agreed-upon algorithms and keys. This encryption protects the data from being read by unauthorized parties during transmission.

3. Certificate Verification: SSL/TLS uses digital certificates to authenticate the identity of the server, ensuring that users are connecting to legitimate websites.

VPNs (Virtual Private Networks): It creates a secure, encrypted tunnel between a user's device and a remote server. This tunnel encrypts all data transmitted between the device and the server, providing privacy and security even on unsecured networks, such as public Wi-Fi.

How VPNs Work:

1. Connection Establishment: When a user connects to a VPN, their device establishes a secure connection with the VPN server.

2. Data Encryption: All data transmitted between the user's device and the VPN server is encrypted, protecting it from eavesdropping and interception.

3. IP Address Masking: VPNs mask the user's IP address, making it more difficult for websites and other entities to track their online activities.

Email Encryption: Email encryption protects the content of email messages from unauthorized access. There are several methods for encrypting email:

1. PGP (Pretty Good Privacy): A widely used method for encrypting email content and attachments. PGP uses a combination of symmetric and asymmetric encryption to secure messages.

2. S/MIME (Secure/Multipurpose Internet Mail Extensions): A standard that uses digital certificates for authentication and encryption. S/MIME is supported by many email clients and provides strong security for email communication.

These are measures to protect data at rest:

Full Disk Encryption: Full Disk Encryption (FDE) encrypts the entire disk on a device, ensuring that all data stored on it is protected. FDE is commonly used on laptops, desktops, and external drives to safeguard data if the device is lost or stolen.

How FDE Works:

1. Encryption of Disk: The entire disk is encrypted, including the operating system and all files. This ensures that data is inaccessible without the proper decryption key.

2. Authentication: Access to the encrypted disk requires authentication, such as a password or biometric scan. This ensures that only authorized users can access the data.

File-Level Encryption: This encrypts individual files or folders rather than the entire disk. This method allows for selective encryption, providing flexibility in protecting specific data while leaving other data unencrypted.

How File-Level Encryption Works:

1. Selective Encryption: Users can choose which files or folders to encrypt, allowing for granular control over data protection.

2. Decryption of Access: Files are encrypted when stored and decrypted when accessed by authorized users, ensuring that sensitive information is protected at all times.

Database Encryption: It protects data stored in databases from unauthorized access. This can include both encryption of data at rest and encryption of data in transit.

How Database Encryption Works:

1. Data Encryption at Rest: Data stored in the database is encrypted to prevent unauthorized access if the database is compromised.

2. Data Encryption in Transit: Data transmitted between the database and client applications is encrypted to protect it from interception and tampering.

Encryption Best Practices

To maximize the effectiveness of encryption and ensure robust data protection, organizations should adhere to several best practices:

Use Strong Encryption Standards: Always use strong and up-to-date encryption algorithms and standards. For symmetric encryption, AES-256 is recommended for its high level of security. For asymmetric encryption, RSA with a key length of at least 2048 bits or ECC with appropriate key lengths provides robust protection.

Secure Key Management: Proper management of encryption keys is crucial for maintaining data security and involves several key practices. Key generation should be performed using secure methods to ensure that keys are of sufficient length and strength. Once generated, key storage must be handled with care, utilizing hardware security modules (HSMs) or other secure methods to protect the keys from unauthorized access. Then, key rotation is essential; regularly updating and changing encryption keys helps to mitigate the risks associated with potential key compromise and ensures ongoing protection of encrypted data. Access control will restrict access to encryption keys to authorized personnel only.

Regularly Update and Patch Systems: Keep all systems and software up to date with the latest security patches and updates. This practice helps address vulnerabilities that could be exploited to compromise encryption.

Implement Layered Security: It should be part of a broader security strategy that includes other measures, such as firewalls, intrusion detection systems (IDS), and secure authentication methods. A layered approach ensures comprehensive protection against various threats.

Educate Users and Stakeholders: Educate users and stakeholders about encryption practices and the importance of data protection. Training should cover secure handling of encrypted data, recognizing phishing attempts, and best practices for maintaining data confidentiality.

To illustrate the practical application of encryption, consider the following case studies. In 2017, Equifax experienced a massive data breach that exposed sensitive information to approximately 147 million individuals. The breach was attributed to a vulnerability in a web application, which could have been mitigated by robust encryption practices. This case underscores the importance of implementing strong encryption to protect sensitive data and avoid costly breaches. The second example is WhatsApp End-to-End Encryption method. This employs end-to-end encryption to protect the privacy of its users' messages. This encryption ensures that only the sender and recipient can read the messages, even if intercepted during transmission. The use of this method highlights the effectiveness of strong encryption in safeguarding communication and maintaining user privacy.

Advancements in encryption technology are crucial for addressing emerging threats and enhancing data security. Post-quantum encryption is a key area of research aimed at developing cryptographic algorithms resilient to the potential future capabilities of quantum computers, ensuring data security as quantum technology evolves. Homomorphic encryption represents another significant advancement, allowing computations to be performed on encrypted data without requiring decryption, thereby enhancing data privacy in cloud computing and other applications. Blockchain technology utilizes cryptographic principles to secure and validate transactions, and its integration with encryption can further strengthen data protection by providing transparent, immutable records of data exchanges. These advancements collectively contribute to a more robust and future-proof approach to data security.

Encryption is a powerful tool for protecting online privacy and data, both in transit and at rest. By understanding and implementing encryption practices, organizations and individuals can safeguard sensitive information from unauthorized access and breaches. From securing communications and files to protecting data in databases, encryption plays a vital role in modern cybersecurity. As technology continues to advance, staying informed about encryption trends and best practices will be essential for maintaining holistic data security and privacy.

CHAPTER FOUR

THE ROLE OF PERSONAL FIREWALLS AND ANTIVIRUS SOFTWARE

Personal firewalls and antivirus software are core components of any comprehensive cybersecurity strategy. They serve as the first line of defense against various types of cyber threats, including malware, unauthorized access, and network intrusions. We will explore the role of personal firewalls and antivirus software in safeguarding digital environments, detailing their functions, benefits, limitations, and best practices for effective use.

What are Personal Firewalls

A personal firewall is a software application or hardware device designed to monitor and control incoming and outgoing network traffic based on predetermined security rules. It acts as a barrier between a user's device and the external network, filtering data to prevent unauthorized access and mitigate potential threats. They operate by examining network packets units of data transmitted over a network and comparing them to a set of security rules. When a packet meets the criteria defined by these rules, it is either allowed to pass through or is blocked.

Personal firewalls typically function at two primary levels. Packet Filtering, which is a method, involves inspecting data packets based on predefined rules such as IP addresses, port numbers, and protocols. Packets that do not meet the criteria are blocked. The second level is Stateful Inspection. This more advanced method tracks the state of active connections and uses this information to determine whether a packet is part of an established connection or if it is suspicious.

It also include features such as application control which restricts or permits network access for specific applications based on their behavior and requirements. It also has intrusion detection and prevention which monitors network traffic for signs of malicious activity and takes action to block or alert users of potential threats.

There are several key benefits to employing personal firewalls.

Protection against Unauthorized Access: By filtering incoming and outgoing traffic, personal firewalls help prevent unauthorized users from accessing sensitive data or systems.

Mitigation of Malware and Viruses: They can block known malware and viruses from entering the system, reducing the risk of infection.

Enhanced Privacy: Personal firewalls can help protect personal information from being transmitted without consent, enhancing user privacy.

Customizable Security Rules: Users can tailor firewall rules to their specific needs and preferences, providing a flexible security solution.

There are limitations of personal firewalls despite their advantages.

Not a Complete Security Solution: Firewalls alone cannot protect against all types of cyber threats, such as phishing attacks or social engineering.

Potential for False Positives: Overly stringent firewall rules can block legitimate traffic, potentially disrupting normal operations.

Performance Impact: Some personal firewalls can affect system performance, especially if they are not configured properly or if they inspect a large volume of network traffic.

Exploring Antivirus Software

Antivirus software is designed to detect, prevent, and remove malicious software, commonly referred to as malware. This includes viruses, worms, Trojans, ransomware, and spyware. Antivirus software operates by scanning files and programs for known signatures of malware or by using behavioral analysis to identify suspicious activity.

They use several techniques to detect and neutralize threats. Signature-based detection is the traditional approach, where the software scans files for known malware signatures such as specific patterns or strings of data linked to recognized threats. In contrast, heuristic-based detection involves analyzing the behavior and characteristics of files and programs to uncover new or unknown malware by recognizing suspicious patterns or actions. Behavioral-based detection monitors the real-time behavior of programs, looking for malicious activities or anomalies that might suggest the presence of malware while sandboxing is a technique used by some antivirus solutions to isolate and execute potentially harmful files in a controlled environment, allowing the software to observe their behavior without impacting the rest of the system.

Antivirus software offers several critical benefits:

Protection against Malware: Antivirus software helps detect and remove a wide range of malware, including viruses, worms, and ransomware.

Real-Time Scanning: Continuous scanning of files and programs helps to identify and mitigate threats as they emerge, providing ongoing protection.

System Optimization: Many antivirus programs include features to optimize system performance by cleaning up unnecessary files and managing system resources.

Email and Web Protection: Advanced antivirus solutions often include protection for email and web browsing, helping to block malicious attachments and websites.

However, antivirus software is not without its drawbacks:

Dependence on Signatures: Signature-based detection relies on known malware signatures, which means it may not detect new or unknown threats until they are added to the database.

Performance Impact. Scanning processes can slow down system performance, especially on lower-end devices or when scanning large volumes of data.

False Positives: Antivirus software can sometimes identify legitimate files or programs as threats, leading to potential disruptions or the need for manual intervention.

For optimal protection, personal firewalls and antivirus software should be used in conjunction. Each provides complementary security functions that together create a more robust defense against cyber threats. Their integration offers several advantages. Integrating a firewall with antivirus software creates a layered security approach that addresses both network-level and file-level threats. This combination ensures comprehensive threat detection, with firewalls focusing on blocking network-based threats while antivirus software targets malicious files and programs. By employing both tools, users benefit from a multifaceted defense strategy that reduces the likelihood of successful attacks and enhances overall security posture.

To achieve effective integration, it is essential to follow several processes. First, keep the software updated by regularly installing the latest threat definitions and security patches for both tools. Next, configure properly to ensure that the firewall and antivirus software work harmoniously without conflicting, and adjust their settings as needed to optimize both performance and protection. Additionally, monitor alerts and logs consistently, reviewing the security notifications and logs from both tools to detect and respond to potential threats promptly. Finally, conduct regular scans with the antivirus software to identify and address any malware infections or vulnerabilities, ensuring ongoing protection for your system.

Choosing the Right Tools

Selecting the appropriate personal firewall and antivirus software is crucial for effective protection. This will ensure you get the right protection tailored for your operations.

When choosing a personal firewall, evaluate the following features:

- Ease of Use: Look for a firewall that is user-friendly and offers a straightforward interface for configuring rules and settings.

- Customization Options: Choose a firewall that allows for granular control over security rules and application permissions.

- Performance Impact: Opt for a firewall that minimizes system performance impact while providing robust security features.

- When selecting antivirus software, consider these aspects:

- Detection Capabilities: Consider antivirus software with strong detection capabilities, including signature-based, heuristic, and behavioral analysis.

- System Compatibility: Ensure that the antivirus software is compatible with your operating system and does not significantly affect system performance.

Additional Features: Consider additional features such as web protection, email scanning, and system optimization tools.

Analyzing real-world cases can offer valuable insights into how effective personal firewalls and antivirus software truly are. The WannaCry ransomware attack in 2017 highlighted the importance of having robust security measures in place. The ransomware exploited vulnerabilities in unpatched systems, encrypting files and demanding ransom payments. Personal firewalls and updated antivirus software could have mitigated the impact by blocking the malware and preventing its spread. In 2013, Target experienced a data breach that exposed the personal and financial information of millions of customers. The breach was facilitated by compromised network access credentials. A well-configured personal firewall could have provided an additional layer of protection by blocking unauthorized access attempts and monitoring network traffic.

These are examples that aid us in understanding the need for employing these strategies.

Future advancements in threat detection will leverage artificial intelligence (AI) and machine learning to identify and respond to sophisticated threats in real-time, significantly improving the detection of new and unknown malware and enhancing overall security effectiveness. As cloud computing continues to grow, personal firewalls and antivirus software will integrate more seamlessly with cloud-based security solutions, offering enhanced protection for data stored in the cloud. Additionally, future developments will focus on improving user experience by minimizing system performance impacts, reducing false positives, and providing more intuitive interfaces for managing security settings.

Personal firewalls and antivirus software are essential tools for protecting against a wide range of cyber threats. By understanding their functions, benefits, and limitations, users can effectively safeguard their digital environments and mitigate risks. Integrating these tools, selecting the right solutions, and following the best practices will contribute to a robust cybersecurity strategy. As technology continues to advance, staying informed about emerging trends and improvements in personal firewalls and antivirus software will be crucial for maintaining strong data security and privacy.

CHAPTER FIVE

SOCIAL ENGINEERING AND PHISHING

In maintaining a secure framework, it is imperative to recognize and defend against deceptive tactics. One of such is social engineering and phishing which emerge as particularly dangerous threats to both individuals and organizations. Unlike technical attacks that target software flaws, these methods prey on human psychology and behavior. We will explore the complexities of social engineering and phishing, detailing their techniques, effects, and defensive strategies. Gaining insight into these manipulative tactics is essential in our quest to safeguard online privacy and data.

Social Engineering

Social engineering refers to a range of manipulative techniques used to deceive individuals into divulging confidential information or performing actions that compromise security. Unlike brute-force attacks or malware, social engineering attacks target the human element, leveraging psychological manipulation rather than technical vulnerabilities.

There are several common techniques employed by actors to carry out social engineering. Pretexting involves crafting a fabricated scenario, known as the "pretext," to trick a target into divulging information. For instance, an attacker might impersonate an IT support technician, requesting login credentials under the pretense of performing routine maintenance. On the other hand, baiting works by presenting something appealing to lure victims into a trap. This might take the form of a tempting free download, a prize, or a seemingly innocuous USB drive left in a public area. Once the victim takes the bait, they may inadvertently install malicious software or reveal personal information.

Tailgating, also known as "piggybacking," involves an attacker gaining unauthorized physical access to a secure area by following an authorized person through a restricted door or entry point. Similarly, attackers might employ seemingly harmless quizzes or surveys to collect personal information from targets. This data can then be used to answer security questions or build a profile for future attacks. Another method is impersonation, where attackers pose as individuals with authority or trusted entities to deceive victims into revealing sensitive information. For example, they might pretend to be a high-ranking executive in order to solicit confidential data from an employee. These are several means to which unauthorized entrance can be gained into security frameworks.

The psychological principles behind social engineering exploit human behaviors and cognitive biases, such as authority, reciprocity, and urgency, to manipulate individuals into disclosing sensitive information or performing actions that compromise security. Let us briefly understand how these biases are exploited.

1. Reciprocity: People are more likely to comply with requests from someone who has previously done something for them. Attackers may exploit this principle by first providing a small favor before making a more significant request.

2. Authority: Individuals tend to follow instructions from perceived authorities. Attackers often exploit this by impersonating figures of authority, such as company executives or law enforcement officers.

3. Scarcity: The perception of scarcity can increase an item's perceived value. Attackers may use urgent or limited time offers to rush victims into making hasty decisions without proper scrutiny.

4. Social Proof: Individuals often look at others to guide their actions. Social engineers may exploit this by pretending to be part of a group or by creating fake testimonials to validate their credibility.

5. Trust: Building trust is fundamental to social engineering. Attackers may establish rapport with targets, gaining their confidence before making malicious requests.

6. Urgency: This refers to the psychological pressure to act quickly, often driven by the perception of an imminent threat or limited time, which can lead individuals to make hasty decisions without thorough consideration or verification.

Phishing: An Overview

Phishing is a specific type of social engineering attack where attackers attempt to deceive individuals into providing sensitive information or performing actions that compromise security. It typically involves fraudulent emails, websites, or messages that appear legitimate but are designed to steal personal information.

Email phishing is the most prevalent type of phishing attack, where fraudulent emails are sent that appear to originate from legitimate sources. These emails typically include malicious links or attachments designed to steal login credentials, install malware, or gather personal information. In contrast, spear phishing targets specific individuals or organizations with highly personalized messages, often after thorough research, to make the communications seem more credible and relevant. Whaling, a subtype of spear phishing, focuses on high-profile individuals such as executives or senior officials. These attacks are more sophisticated and convincing, reflecting the higher stakes involved in deceiving influential targets.

Smishing, or SMS phishing, occurs when attackers send fraudulent text messages with links or requests for personal information, often masquerading as legitimate organizations like banks or service providers. Vishing, or voice phishing, involves using phone calls to trick victims into disclosing sensitive information. Attackers may impersonate trusted figures such as bank representatives or government officials to gather personal data. Pharming redirects users from legitimate websites to fraudulent ones, usually by exploiting vulnerabilities in domain name system (DNS) servers or infecting a user's computer with malware that alters DNS settings.

A first step in guarding against this tactic is by looking out for several indicators. Recognizing phishing attempts can be challenging, as attackers continuously refine their methods. However, certain signs can help identify potential phishing attacks:

Suspicious Sender Addresses: Check for discrepancies in the email address or phone number of the sender. These emails may use addresses that resemble legitimate ones but contain subtle differences.

Unusual Requests: Be wary of unsolicited requests for sensitive information, especially if they involve urgent or unexpected actions, such as changing passwords or verifying account details.

Grammar and Spelling Errors: Many phishing messages contain errors in spelling, grammar, or formatting. While not all attempts contain these mistakes, their presence can be a red flag.

Unexpected Attachments or Links: Avoid opening attachments or clicking links in unsolicited messages. Hover over links to verify their destination before clicking.

Urgent or Threatening Language: These attempts often use alarming language to create a sense of urgency. Be cautious of messages that threaten account suspension or immediate action.

Unusual Requests for Personal Information: Legitimate organizations typically do not request sensitive information via email or text. Be cautious if asked to provide personal details, such as Social Security numbers or account passwords.

Defending Against Social Engineering and Phishing

To achieve optimal results, a multi-faceted approach that includes awareness, technical measures, and good practices is required. Here are strategies to bolster your defenses:

Awareness and Training

Educate yourself and others: Understanding the tactics and signs of social engineering and phishing is crucial. Regularly educate yourself and others within your organization about emerging threats and best practices.

Conduct Training and Simulations: Organizations should conduct regular training and simulations to prepare employees for potential social engineering attacks. These exercises can help individuals recognize and respond to phishing attempts effectively.

Promote a Culture of Security: Foster a culture of security awareness where employees feel comfortable reporting suspicious activities without fear of reprimand.

Technical Measures

Implement Email Filters and Security Software: Use advanced email filters to detect and block phishing emails. Ensure that security software, including antivirus and anti-malware tools, is up-to-date and configured to detect phishing attempts.

Utilize Multi-Factor Authentication (MFA): MFA adds an additional layer of security by requiring more than one form of verification before granting access. Even if login credentials are compromised, MFA can prevent unauthorized access.

Regularly Update Software and Systems: Keeping software, operating systems, and applications up-to-date helps protect against vulnerabilities that attackers might exploit for phishing and social engineering attacks.

Monitor for Suspicious Activity: Implement monitoring solutions to detect unusual or unauthorized access attempts. Regularly review logs and alerts for signs of potential breaches.

Best Practices

Verify Requests Independently: Always verify requests for sensitive information through a separate communication channel. If you receive a request via email or text, confirm its legitimacy by contacting the requester directly through known contact methods.

Be Cautious with Personal Information: Limit the amount of personal information shared online. Be mindful of the information you provide on social media, as attackers may use it to craft convincing phishing attacks.

Use Strong and Unique Passwords: Create strong, unique passwords for each of your accounts. Avoid using easily guessable passwords or reusing the same password across multiple sites.

Be Skeptical of Unsolicited Communications: Approach unsolicited communications with caution. Verify the authenticity of any unexpected messages, especially those that request sensitive information or prompt urgent actions.

Regularly Back Up Important Data: Maintain regular backups of important data to mitigate the impact of potential ransomware attacks or data loss resulting from phishing attempts.

Now, attacks can occur, and it is important to know how to respond to them effectively. In response to an attack, it is crucial to immediately report any suspicious activity or suspected phishing attempts to your organization's IT or security team, as swift reporting can help mitigate damage and prevent further incidents. Following an attack, it is essential to review and update security protocols to address any vulnerabilities that were exploited. Conducting a thorough post-incident analysis will help identify lessons learned and enhance future defenses. Additionally, if sensitive information has been compromised, take steps to secure the affected accounts and data, reassess your overall security posture, and implement additional measures as necessary to safeguard against future incidents.

Safeguarding social engineering and phishing is crucial in the broader context of online privacy and data protection because these tactics exploit human vulnerabilities to bypass technical security measures. While advanced encryption, secure networks, and robust software defenses are essential, they can be undermined if attackers successfully manipulate individuals into disclosing sensitive information or performing actions that compromise security. By addressing social engineering and phishing, organizations and individuals strengthen their overall security posture, ensuring that their privacy and data protection strategies are comprehensive and resilient against both technical and psychological threats. This holistic approach helps prevent unauthorized access, data breaches, and identity theft, thereby safeguarding personal and organizational information from a wide range of potential threats.

CHAPTER SIX

THE IMPACT OF BIG DATA: BALANCING INNOVATION AND PRIVACY

"Big Data" has become synonymous with progress and innovation. Organizations across various industries are harnessing vast amounts of data to drive insights, enhance decision-making, and fuel technological advancements. However, as the volume and complexity of data grow, so too do concerns about privacy and data protection. This chapter delves into the intricate balance between leveraging big data for innovation and safeguarding individual privacy, exploring the challenges, implications, and strategies necessary to navigate this complex landscape.

What Is Big Data

Big data refers to the vast and diverse sets of information generated from various sources, including social media, sensors, transactional systems, and more. It is characterized by its volume, velocity, variety, and veracity, often summarized as the

"4 V's" of big data. The ability to analyze and derive meaningful insights from such extensive datasets has transformative potential across multiple sectors.

The characteristics of big data are defined by its immense scale and rapid pace. Volume refers to the vast amounts of data generated every second, ranging from petabytes to exabytes. This includes diverse sources such as social media posts, transaction records, and sensor outputs. Velocity, on the other hand, captures the unprecedented speed at which data is produced and processed. The continuous stream of real-time data from various sources, including devices, social media, and online transactions, necessitates swift and efficient analysis to derive valuable insights.

Variety in big data refers to the diverse types of data it encompasses, including structured data like databases, semi-structured data such as JSON files, and unstructured data including text, video, and audio. This wide range of data formats requires effective integration and analysis techniques. Veracity highlights the importance of ensuring data accuracy and reliability. Since big data often integrates information from various sources, it is essential to address the varying levels of quality and consistency to maintain the integrity of the insights derived.

The promise of big data lies in its potential to drive transformative advancements and deliver substantial benefits across various sectors. By harnessing vast and diverse datasets, organizations can unlock new insights and innovations that have the power to reshape industries and improve lives. Some of the sectors have felt the impact and use of big data in driving efficiency in their activities.

Healthcare: In healthcare, big data enables personalized medicine by analyzing patient records, genetic information, and treatment outcomes. This can lead to more accurate diagnoses, tailored treatments, and improved patient care.

Finance: Financial institutions leverage big data for risk management, fraud detection, and customer segmentation. Predictive analytics can enhance investment strategies and optimize trading decisions.

Retail: Retailers use big data to understand consumer behavior, personalize marketing efforts, and manage inventory more effectively. Insights from purchase patterns and online interactions help tailor products and promote individual preferences.

Transportation: Big data analytics improve transportation systems by optimizing routes, predicting maintenance needs, and enhancing traffic management. This contributes to more efficient and safer transportation networks.

Smart Cities: Big data supports the development of smart cities by integrating data from various sensors and systems to improve urban planning, energy management, and public safety.

Education: Big data enhances educational outcomes by enabling personalized learning experiences. Analyzing student performance data allows educators to tailor teaching methods, identify learning gaps, and provide targeted support to improve student engagement and achievement.

Agriculture: In agriculture, big data facilitates precision farming by integrating data from soil sensors, weather forecasts, and crop performance. This enables farmers to optimize resource use, increase crop yields, and manage pests and diseases more effectively, leading to more sustainable agricultural practices.

Energy: The energy sector benefits from big data through improved grid management and energy efficiency. Analyzing data from smart meters, energy consumption patterns, and environmental factors helps utilities optimize energy distribution, forecast demand, and implement strategies for reducing energy waste and supporting renewable energy integration.

Privacy Concerns in the Age of Big Data

Despite the advantages, big data raises substantial privacy concerns. The collection, storage, and analysis of massive datasets often involve personal and sensitive information, leading to potential risks.

Many big data applications involve collecting extensive personal information, often without explicit consent or full transparency. Users may unknowingly agree to data collection through broad privacy policies or default settings. Additionally, data collected by one organization can be shared with or sold to third parties, potentially leading to misuse or unauthorized access, often without clear communication to the individuals involved. Furthermore, large datasets are prime targets for cybercriminals, and data breaches can expose sensitive personal information, resulting in identity theft, financial loss, and reputational damage.

The ability to analyze large volumes of data can lead to intrusive surveillance and profiling, where detailed insights into individuals' behaviors and preferences might be used for manipulation or discrimination. Additionally, aggregating data from multiple sources can result in unintended privacy invasions, as even anonymized data may sometimes be re-identified when combined with other datasets.

To address privacy concerns, several regulatory frameworks and standards have been established to guide the responsible use of big data. The General Data Protection Regulation (GDPR), implemented by the European Union, provides a comprehensive approach to data protection, emphasizing transparency, consent, and individuals' rights to access and control their data. The Health Insurance Portability and Accountability Act (HIPAA) sets standards for the privacy and security of medical records and personal health information in the United States, ensuring the protection of sensitive health data. The Children's Online Privacy Protection Act (COPPA) regulates the collection of personal information from children under the age of 13, requiring parental consent and imposing specific requirements on online services aimed at children. Additionally, the Data Protection Act (DPA), implemented in various countries, outlines guidelines for data processing and protection, including provisions for data security, consent, and individuals' rights, to provide a consistent approach to data privacy across different jurisdictions.

Industry standards play a crucial role in guiding ethical data management and ensuring the protection of privacy in big data environments. The ISO/IEC 27001 standard provides a comprehensive framework for establishing, implementing, maintaining, and continuously improving an information security management system (ISMS), helping organizations systematically manage and safeguard sensitive data. ISO/IEC 27701 extends this framework by focusing specifically on privacy information management, offering guidelines for implementing privacy controls and ensuring compliance with privacy regulations. The Fair Information Practice Principles (FIPPs), established by various authorities, provide foundational guidelines for privacy practices, emphasizing transparency, data minimization, and individual participation to guide the ethical collection and use of big data.

Balancing Innovation and Privacy

Striking a balance between harnessing the potential of big data and protecting privacy requires a thoughtful approach. Organizations must implement strategies to mitigate privacy risks while maximizing the benefits of data-driven innovation.

Privacy by Design

Incorporating privacy considerations into the design and development of big data systems is essential. Privacy by design involves embedding privacy features into the architecture of systems and processes, ensuring that privacy is a core consideration rather than an afterthought.

Data Minimization: Collect only the data necessary for specific purposes. Avoid collecting excessive or unrelated information that increases the risk of privacy breaches.

Anonymization and Pseudonymization: Use techniques to anonymize or pseudonymize data, reducing the risk of identifying individuals in datasets. While not foolproof, these methods can help protect privacy while still allowing for valuable analysis.

Access Controls: Implement strict access controls to limit who can view or handle sensitive data. Ensure that only authorized personnel have access to personal information.

Transparency and Consent: Clearly communicate data collection practices and obtain informed consent from individuals. Provide options for users to control their data and opt-out of data collection where possible.

Data Security: Employ robust security measures to protect data from unauthorized access, breaches, and cyber threats. This includes encryption, secure storage, and regular security assessments.

Ethical Data Use

Ethical considerations should guide the use of big data to ensure that it benefits individuals and society without causing harm. This involves:

Fairness: Avoid using data in ways that discriminate or unfairly impact individuals or groups. Ensure that data-driven decisions are equitable and just.

Accountability: Hold organizations accountable for their data practices. Establish mechanisms for addressing grievances and ensuring compliance with privacy standards.

Impact Assessments: Conduct privacy impact assessments (PIAs) to evaluate the potential effects of data collection and use on individuals' privacy. Address any identified risks and mitigate potential negative impacts.

Public Awareness: Promote public awareness of data practices and privacy rights. Educate individuals about how their data is used and how they can protect their privacy.

Some circumstances that have occurred which highlights the risks of big data misuse we can relate with are the Cambridge Analytica scandal. The political consulting firm harvested personal data from millions of Facebook users without their consent and used it for targeted political advertising. The incident raised significant concerns about data privacy, consent, and the ethical use of personal information. Google has faced controversies related to its use of artificial intelligence (AI) and big data, including issues of bias and privacy. The company's approach to AI ethics and data handling has sparked debates about transparency, accountability, and the impact of data-driven technologies on society.

As technology and data analytics evolve, new challenges and opportunities will arise. The integration of Artificial Intelligence (AI) and Machine Learning (ML) with big data promises to enhance data analysis capabilities, but it also introduces new privacy concerns and ethical considerations, particularly around automated decision-making and algorithmic biases. Data sovereignty will gain significance as countries seek to control data within their borders, potentially leading to regulations that impact how data is stored, processed, and transferred across international boundaries. Blockchain technology presents potential solutions for improving data security and privacy through decentralized and transparent management. Its application in big data contexts could address some privacy issues while facilitating secure data sharing. Enhanced Privacy Technologies such as differential privacy and secure multi-party computation, will provide new ways to protect individuals' data while enabling valuable analysis.

Balancing the innovative potential of big data with the imperative of protecting privacy is a complex and ongoing challenge. By understanding the implications of big data, implementing robust privacy measures, and adhering to ethical principles, organizations and individuals can navigate this niche effectively.

As technology continues to advance, a proactive and thoughtful approach to data privacy and protection will be essential in ensuring that big data serves as a tool for positive change rather than a source of privacy risks.

CHAPTER SEVEN

PRIVACY SETTINGS

Securing online accounts is critical due to the vast amount of personal information stored and transmitted through digital platforms. This includes sensitive data such as financial details, health information, and personal communications. A compromised account can lead to a range of issues, from unauthorized transactions and identity theft to reputational damage and emotional distress. By proactively managing privacy settings and implementing robust security measures, individuals can protect themselves from these risks and preserve their digital privacy.

With cyber threats becoming increasingly sophisticated, understanding and effectively managing privacy settings is essential to safeguarding your digital footprint. This chapter explores the importance of securing online accounts, provides a comprehensive guide to privacy settings across various platforms, and demonstrates practical steps to enhance account security.

Understanding Privacy Settings

Privacy settings are tools provided by online platforms that allow users to control who can access their information and how it is shared. These settings vary depending on the platform but generally include options for managing visibility, controlling data sharing, and setting permissions for third-party applications. Understanding and customizing these settings is essential for protecting personal data and ensuring that only authorized parties can access it.

Key Privacy Settings across Platforms

Social media: Social media platforms like Facebook, Instagram, and Twitter offer extensive privacy settings to control who can view your posts, friend requests, and personal information. Options include adjusting your profile visibility, managing post audiences, and setting preferences for tagging and location sharing.

Email: Email providers such as Gmail and Outlook offer privacy settings to manage account access, filter spam, and control data sharing. Key settings include two-factor authentication (2FA), account recovery options, and permissions for third-party applications.

Online Banking: Online banking platforms provide privacy settings to manage account security, transaction alerts, and data sharing preferences. Settings include account login security, transaction notifications, and the ability to review and manage authorized devices.

E-commerce: E-commerce sites like Amazon and eBay offer privacy settings to control data sharing with vendors, manage order history visibility, and set preferences for marketing communications. Key settings include managing saved payment methods and adjusting email preferences.

Cloud Services: Cloud storage services such as Google Drive and Dropbox provide settings for controlling file sharing, managing access permissions, and securing data with encryption. Options include sharing settings, link access controls, and security alerts.

Practical Ways to Secure Your Online Accounts

To effectively secure your online accounts, follow these practical steps to enhance your privacy and protect your personal information:

1. Use Strong and Unique Passwords: Creating strong, unique passwords for each of your online accounts is a fundamental step in securing your digital presence. A strong password typically includes a mix of uppercase and lowercase letters, numbers, and special characters. Avoid using easily guessable information, such as birthdays or common words. Consider using a passphrase—a sequence of unrelated words combined into a longer password—to improve security.

Example:

- Weak Password: `Password123`
- Strong Password: `G$7pL9#xQ!2f`

2. Enable Two-Factor Authentication (2FA): Two-factor authentication (2FA) adds an additional layer of security by requiring a second form of verification in addition to your password. This typically involves receiving a one-time code via SMS, email, or an authenticator app. Enabling 2FA significantly reduces the risk of unauthorized access, even if your password is compromised.

How to Enable 2FA:

- Gmail: Go to Google Account Settings > Security > 2-Step Verification and follow the setup instructions.

- Facebook: Go to Settings & Privacy > Settings > Security and Login > Use two-factor authentication.

3. Review and Adjust Privacy Settings Regularly: Regularly reviewing and updating your privacy settings ensures that your personal information remains protected as platforms and their features evolve. Check the privacy settings for each platform you use and adjust them according to your current needs and preferences.

How to Review Privacy Settings:

- Instagram: Go to Settings > Privacy and Security to manage account visibility and interaction preferences.

- Amazon: Go to Accounts & Lists > Your Account > Login & Security to review and update security settings.

4. Monitor Account Activity and Alerts: Many platforms provide tools to monitor account activity and receive alerts for suspicious behavior. Regularly reviewing these alerts and activity logs can help you detect potential security issues early and take appropriate action.

How to Monitor Account Activity:

- Banking: Check your account statements and transaction history regularly for unauthorized transactions.

- Social media: Review recent logins and activity logs to spot any unfamiliar access.

5. Manage App Permissions and Data Sharing: Control which third-party applications and services have access to your accounts and data. Regularly review app permissions and revoke access for any applications that are no longer needed or appear suspicious.

How to Manage App Permissions:

- Google Account: Go to Security > Third-party apps with account access to review and manage permissions.

- Facebook: Go to Settings & Privacy > Settings > Apps and Websites to manage app permissions.

6. Use Secure Connections: When accessing your accounts, ensure that you are using secure connections. Avoid logging in to sensitive accounts on public Wi-Fi networks and always look for "HTTPS" in the URL to verify that the connection is encrypted.

How to Ensure Secure Connections:

- Browser: Look for a padlock icon in the address bar and "HTTPS" in the URL before entering login credentials.

- VPN: Use a Virtual Private Network (VPN) to secure your internet connection and protect your data when using public networks.

7. Backup and Encrypt Important Data: Backing up important data ensures that you can recover it in case of a security breach or data loss. Additionally, encrypting sensitive data adds an extra layer of protection by making it unreadable to unauthorized users.

How to Backup and Encrypt Data:

- Cloud Storage: Use services like Google Drive or Dropbox to regularly back up important files.

- Encryption: Use tools like VeraCrypt or BitLocker to encrypt sensitive files and folders on your computer.

8. Educate Yourself About Phishing and Scams: Awareness of common phishing tactics and scams can help you avoid falling victim to malicious attempts to gain access to your accounts. Be cautious of unsolicited emails, messages, or calls requesting personal information or login credentials.

How to Recognize Phishing:

- Email: Check for suspicious sender addresses, unexpected attachments, and urgent or threatening language.

- Links: Hover over links to verify their destination before clicking.

9. Secure Your Devices: Ensuring that your devices are secure is crucial for protecting your online accounts. Install reputable antivirus software, keep your operating system and applications up-to-date, and enable device encryption where possible.

How to Secure Devices:

- Antivirus: Use antivirus software to scan for and remove malware.

- Updates: Regularly update your operating system and applications to patch security vulnerabilities.

10. Enable Account Recovery Options: Setting up account recovery options, such as backup email addresses or phone numbers, ensures that you can regain access to your accounts if you forget your password or lose access. Keep these options current and secure.

How to Enable Account Recovery:

- Gmail: Go to Google Account Settings > Security > Ways we can verify it's you to set up recovery options.

- Facebook: Go to Settings & Privacy > Settings > Security and Login > Setting up extra security to add recovery methods.

Demonstrating Practical Steps: Securing Your Online Accounts

We will delve into a practical guide on how to secure samples of online accounts.

Securing a Gmail Account

1. Set a Strong Password:

    - Go to Google Account Settings.

    - Select Security > Password.

    - Enter a new, strong password and confirm it.

2. Enable Two-Factor Authentication:

   - Go to Google Account Settings.

   - Select Security > 2-Step Verification.

   - Follow the prompts to set up 2FA using your phone or authenticator app.

3. Review Account Activity:

   - Go to Google Account Settings.

   - Select Security > Recent security events.

   - Review recent login attempts and activities for any suspicious behavior.

4. Manage App Permissions:

   - Go to Google Account Settings.

   - Select Security > Third-party apps with account access.

   - Review and remove any apps that are no longer needed or appear suspicious.

5. Update Recovery Options:

   - Go to Google Account Settings.

   - Select Security > Ways we can verify it's you.

- Add or update your recovery phone number and email address.

Securing a Facebook Account

1. Adjust Privacy Settings:

   - Go to Facebook Settings.

   - Select Privacy > Your Activity.

   - Adjust settings to control who can see your posts and friend requests.

2. Enable Two-Factor Authentication:

   - Go to Facebook Settings.

   - Select Security and Login > Use two-factor authentication.

   - Follow the instructions to set up 2FA using your phone.

3. Review Account Activity:

   - Go to Facebook Settings.

   - Select Security and Login > Where you're logged in.

   - Review active sessions and log out of any that are unfamiliar.

4. Manage App Permissions:

   - Go to Facebook Settings.

   - Select Apps and Websites.

   - Review and remove any apps that you no longer use or do not trust.

5. Set Up Account Recovery:

   - Go to Facebook Settings.

   - Select Security and Login > Setting up extra security.

   - Add backup contact information and recovery options.

Securing your online shopping account

1. Set a Strong and Unique Password: Create a password with a mix of uppercase and lowercase letters, numbers, and special characters, avoiding easily guessable information.

2. Enable Two-Factor Authentication (2FA): Add an extra layer of security by setting up 2FA, choosing either SMS or an authenticator app for the second verification step.

3. Review and Update Account Information: Regularly check and update your personal and payment details to ensure they are accurate and secure.

4. Monitor Order History and Account Activity: Keep an eye on your order history and account activity for any unauthorized transactions and report suspicious activity immediately.

5. Manage App Permissions and Update Software: Review app permissions and ensure your shopping app and browser are updated with the latest security patches.

6. Be Cautious of Phishing Attempts: Verify the authenticity of emails and links before clicking to avoid falling victim to phishing scams.

Securing your online accounts is a proactive and ongoing process that involves understanding and managing privacy settings, using strong authentication methods, and staying vigilant against potential threats. By following the practical steps outlined in this chapter and regularly reviewing your security measures, you can enhance your online privacy and protect your personal information from unauthorized access.

CHAPTER EIGHT

THE INTERNET OF THINGS (IoT): RISKS AND SAFEGUARDS FOR CONNECTED DEVICES

The IoT describes a network of interconnected devices that communicate and share data over the internet, ranging from smart home appliances and wearable devices to industrial sensors and healthcare systems. While it offers remarkable convenience and efficiency, it also introduces significant privacy and security risks. This chapter delves into its intricacies, exploring the risks associated with connected devices and the safeguards necessary to protect online privacy and data. Understanding these elements is crucial to understanding the intricacies of online privacy and data protection where these devices are increasingly prevalent.

From Concept to Reality

The concept of the Internet of Things dates back to the 1990s, but it gained momentum with advancements in wireless technology, cloud computing, and big data analytics. Initially, IoT devices were limited to basic sensors and simple applications. However, as technology evolved, the scope expanded dramatically. Today, IoT encompasses a vast array of devices, from smart thermostats and connected refrigerators to sophisticated industrial machinery and medical implants.

These devices have permeated various aspects of daily life and industry. In smart homes, they control lighting, security systems, and climate settings. Wearable track health metrics such as heart rate and sleep patterns. In industrial settings, sensors monitor equipment performance and predict maintenance needs. In healthcare, they provide remote patient monitoring and enhance diagnostic capabilities. This proliferation of connected devices has transformed how we interact with technology, offering unprecedented convenience but also introducing new privacy and security challenges.

Risks Associated with IoT Devices

The Internet of Things devices, while enhancing convenience and functionality, also present significant risks to privacy and security. These risks arise from vulnerabilities in device design, privacy concerns, compliance, data management practices, and the potential for unauthorized access and misuse.

Data Collection and Storage: They continuously collect and transmit data about users' activities, preferences, and environments. This data, often stored in cloud servers, can reveal sensitive information. For example, a smart thermostat might track daily routines and home occupancy, while a fitness tracker records personal health metrics. Without adequate privacy controls, this data can be accessed by unauthorized parties or misused by the companies managing the devices.

Unauthorized Data Access: Many devices lack robust security measures, making them susceptible to unauthorized access. Vulnerabilities in device firmware, inadequate encryption, and weak authentication mechanisms can expose sensitive data to cybercriminals. For instance, a compromised smart camera could allow hackers to monitor private spaces or access video feeds.

Another privacy concern associated with IoT devices is the potential for data aggregation, where information collected from multiple devices can be combined to create detailed profiles of individuals. For example, data from smart home devices, fitness trackers, and online shopping history can be aggregated to infer personal habits, preferences, and even health conditions, potentially leading to intrusive insights and unauthorized profiling.

Device and Network Exploits: They are often designed with limited security features, focusing on functionality and cost-efficiency rather than robust protection. This design approach can lead to vulnerabilities that attackers exploit. Common vulnerabilities include hardcoded passwords, outdated software, and unsecured communication protocols. Attackers can exploit these weaknesses to gain unauthorized control over devices or disrupt their operations.

Botnet Attacks: Compromised devices are frequently recruited into botnets networks of infected devices controlled by cybercriminals. These botnets can be used to launch Distributed Denial of Service (DDoS) attacks, overwhelming servers or networks with traffic and causing service disruptions.

Insecure APIs: A lot rely on application programming interfaces (APIs) for communication and data exchange. If these APIs are inadequately secured, they can become entry points for attackers. Insecure APIs might expose sensitive data, allow unauthorized control over devices, or be exploited to launch attacks on other connected systems.

Lack of Firmware Updates: They often suffer from outdated firmware, which may contain unpatched vulnerabilities. If manufacturers do not provide regular updates or if users neglect to install them, devices remain susceptible to known exploits. This can leave devices open to attacks that leverage these vulnerabilities, compromising their security and the network they are part of.

Data Ownership and Control: The question of data ownership arises particularly when data is collected and managed by third-party companies. Users may have limited control over how their data is used, shared, or sold. Transparency about data handling practices and user consent are critical ethical considerations that need addressing.

Regulatory Compliance: They must comply with various regulations and standards to ensure data protection and privacy. However, regulatory frameworks are often lagging behind technological advancements, leading to gaps in protection. Companies need to navigate a complex landscape of regulations, which may vary by jurisdiction and industry, to ensure they meet compliance requirements.

Safeguards for IoT Devices

To mitigate the risks associated, implementing robust safeguards is essential for protecting privacy and security. Effective safeguards include strengthening device security, enhancing network protections, and ensuring transparent data handling practices to minimize vulnerabilities and prevent unauthorized access.

Secure Device Design: Manufacturers should prioritize security in the design phase of these devices. This includes implementing strong authentication mechanisms, such as two-factor authentication (2FA), and ensuring that devices use encryption for data transmission and storage. Regular updates and patch management are also essential to address vulnerabilities and enhance security.

User Access Controls: Devices should offer granular access controls, allowing users to manage permissions and restrict access to sensitive features. For example, users should be able to control who can view camera feeds or access personal health data. Implementing user-specific profiles and permissions can help mitigate unauthorized access.

Network Segmentation: Segregating devices from critical systems and data networks can limit the impact of potential security breaches. Network segmentation involves creating separate network zones for different types of devices and applying strict access controls between them. This practice helps contain potential threats and reduces the risk of widespread attacks.

Secure Communication Protocols: They should use secure communication protocols, such as HTTPS or encrypted MQTT (Message Queuing Telemetry Transport), to protect data in transit. Ensuring that communication channels are encrypted helps prevent interception and tampering by malicious actors.

User Consent and Transparency: Users should be informed about the data collection practices and given clear options to consent or opt-out. Privacy policies should be transparent and easy to understand, outlining how data is collected, used, and shared. Providing users with control over their data and ensuring informed consent are crucial for maintaining trust.

Data Minimization and Anonymization: Adopting data minimization practices involves collecting only the data necessary for the device's functionality and avoiding excessive data collection. Anonymizing data where possible helps protect user privacy by ensuring that collected data cannot be traced back to individuals. For example, instead of storing detailed health metrics, a device could store aggregated data to analyze trends without revealing personal information.

Security Audits and Penetration Testing: Conducting frequent security audits and penetration testing helps identify vulnerabilities and assess the effectiveness of security measures. Audits should include device firmware, network configurations, and data handling practices. Penetration testing simulates real-world attacks to evaluate the device's resilience against potential threats.

Firmware Updates and Patches: Regularly updating device firmware and applying security patches are critical for addressing known vulnerabilities and improving device security. Manufacturers should provide timely updates and communicate them to users effectively. Users should ensure that their devices are configured to receive and install updates automatically or manually check for updates periodically.

Securing Personal Devices: Users should implement strong passwords for their IoT devices and change default passwords to prevent unauthorized access. Enabling 2FA where available adds an extra layer of security. Additionally, users should regularly review their device settings and permissions to ensure they align with their privacy preferences.

Monitoring Device Activity: Regularly monitoring device activity helps detect unusual behavior or unauthorized access. Many of these devices offer activity logs or notifications that alert users to potential security issues. Users should review these logs and take action if they notice any suspicious activity.

Educating Yourself and Others: Staying informed about security best practices and emerging threats is essential for maintaining device security. Users should educate themselves and others about the risks associated with these devices and promote good security practices. Participating in online forums, reading security blogs, and attending webinars can provide valuable insights and updates.

The future of IoT security is set to benefit from advancements in technologies such as artificial intelligence (AI) and machine learning (ML), which promise enhanced threat detection and response capabilities. AI-powered security solutions will be able to analyze vast amounts of data in real time, identifying anomalies and potential threats with greater precision. Additionally, blockchain technology is anticipated to provide innovative methods for improving data integrity and security within the ecosystem. Meanwhile, as IoT technology continues to progress, regulatory frameworks will need to evolve to address new privacy and security challenges. Governments and industry bodies are likely to develop updated standards and regulations to ensure that IoT devices comply with rigorous security and privacy requirements. For both manufacturers and users, staying informed about these regulatory changes and ensuring compliance will be essential to maintaining robust protection in an increasingly connected world.

The Internet of Things represents a significant advancement in connectivity and technology, offering numerous benefits across various domains. However, it also introduces complex privacy and security risks that must be carefully managed. By understanding the intricacies of IoT, implementing robust safeguards, and following best practices, users and manufacturers can mitigate these risks and protect sensitive data.

CHAPTER NINE

LEGAL AND ETHICAL CONSIDERATIONS IN DATA COLLECTION AND USAGE

In the age of digital transformation, data has become a central asset for businesses, governments, and individuals alike. As we delve into the complexities of online privacy and data protection, understanding the legal and ethical considerations in data collection and usage is crucial. This chapter explores universal principles and ethical frameworks that guide the collection and use of data, focusing on fundamental concepts that apply globally.

Data privacy refers to the handling, processing, and storage of personal information in ways that protect individuals' rights and freedoms. With the proliferation of digital technologies, personal data is more accessible and valuable than ever before. Ensuring that data is collected and used responsibly is essential for maintaining trust and protecting individuals from potential harm.

Key Legal Principles in Data Protection

Though specific laws vary by region, several universal principles form the foundation of data protection regulations. These principles aim to safeguard personal information and ensure that data collection and usage are carried out in a fair, transparent, and secure manner.

Consent: One of the cornerstones of data protection is the principle of informed consent. Individuals must be aware of and agree to the collection and processing of their personal data. Consent should be given freely, explicitly, and with a clear understanding of how the data will be used. This principle ensures that individuals retain control over their personal information.

Purpose Limitation: Data should only be collected for specific, legitimate purposes. The use of data beyond the original purpose for which it was collected is generally considered a breach of data protection principles. Purpose limitation helps prevent misuse and ensures that data is used in ways that individuals expect and approve.

Data Minimization: The principle of data minimization dictates that only the minimum amount of personal data necessary for the intended purpose should be collected. This reduces the risk of exposure and misuse. Organizations should avoid collecting excessive data and should regularly review their data practices to ensure they align with this principle.

Accuracy: Personal data must be accurate and up to date. Organizations are responsible for ensuring that data is correct and reflecting the current situation of the individual. Inaccurate data can lead to erroneous decisions and unfair treatment, making this principle vital for maintaining fairness and integrity.

Storage Limitation: Data should not be kept for longer than necessary. Organizations must establish retention policies that dictate how long data can be stored and ensure that it is securely deleted once it is no longer needed. This principle helps mitigate risks associated with data breaches and unauthorized access.

Security: The principle of data security requires that personal information is protected against unauthorized access, disclosure, alteration, and destruction. Organizations must implement appropriate technical and organizational measures to safeguard data and ensure its integrity and confidentiality.

Accountability: Organizations are accountable for complying with data protection principles. They must be able to demonstrate that they have implemented effective measures to protect personal data and to ensure that their data handling practices are in line with legal and ethical standards.

Ethical Considerations in Data Collection

Beyond legal requirements, ethical considerations play a crucial role in data collection and usage. These considerations often reflect broader societal values and norms, influencing how data practices are perceived and accepted.

Respect for Privacy: Respecting individuals' privacy is a fundamental ethical principle. This involves not only adhering to legal requirements but also considering the broader implications of data collection practices on individuals' lives. Organizations should strive to avoid intrusions into personal privacy and to handle data with respect and care.

Transparency: Transparency in data collection involves clearly communicating with individuals about how their data will be used, stored, and shared. Ethical practices require that organizations provide clear and accessible information, allowing individuals to make informed decisions about their data.

Fairness: Data collection practices should be fair and equitable. This means avoiding discriminatory practices and ensuring that data usage does not disproportionately impact certain groups or individuals. Fairness also involves giving individuals the ability to review and correct their data if necessary.

Beneficence and Non-Maleficence: Ethical data practices should aim to benefit individuals and society while minimizing harm. Organizations should evaluate the potential benefits and risks associated with data collection and ensure that their practices contribute positively to the public good without causing undue harm.

Informed Choice: Informed choice involves providing individuals with the information and tools they need to make decisions about their data. This includes clear consent processes, accessible privacy policies, and options for individuals to control their data preferences.

Balancing legal and ethical considerations in data collection and usage is fraught with challenges, particularly due to the rapid pace of technological change. As technology evolves swiftly, it frequently outstrips the development of new laws and regulations, leading to gaps in legal protections and ethical standards. This disparity can create a precarious situation where existing legal frameworks may no longer adequately address emerging issues, and ethical norms may struggle to keep pace with technological advancements. Organizations face the complex task of navigating these gaps, striving to align their data practices with both current legal requirements and evolving ethical expectations. They must be proactive in adapting their policies and procedures to ensure that they not only comply with existing laws but also uphold high ethical standards, even as technology continues to advance and introduce new challenges.

Globalization presents another significant challenge in balancing legal and ethical considerations in data collection and usage. In today's interconnected digital environment, data frequently crosses international borders, raising complex questions about which legal and ethical standards apply. Organizations operating on a global scale must navigate a multitude of diverse legal frameworks and cultural expectations, making it crucial to balance compliance with varying local laws while maintaining consistent ethical practices. Additionally, the complexity of data ecosystems, which often involve multiple third-party vendors and data brokers, further complicates the management of ethical data practices. Organizations must carefully manage their relationships with these external entities, ensuring that all parties involved adhere to both legal requirements and ethical standards. This requires vigilant oversight and coordination to ensure that data handling practices remain robust and consistent across all levels of the data system.

To address the challenges of balancing legal and ethical considerations in data collection and usage, organizations can adopt several best practices. Firstly, developing and implementing comprehensive data protection policies is essential. These policies should be designed to reflect both legal requirements and ethical considerations, covering all aspects of data collection, processing, storage, and sharing. By providing clear guidance for employees and stakeholders, organizations ensure that data handling practices are consistent and aligned with established standards. Additionally, conducting regular data protection audits is crucial for maintaining robust data practices. These audits help organizations evaluate their compliance with legal obligations, assess adherence to ethical principles, and measure the effectiveness of their security measures. Through periodic reviews, organizations can identify areas for improvement and make necessary adjustments to enhance their overall data protection framework.

Investing in robust data security measures is vital for protecting personal information. Organizations should prioritize implementing advanced security technologies such as encryption and access controls to safeguard data from unauthorized access and breaches. These measures are essential for maintaining the confidentiality and integrity of personal information in an increasingly digital world. Fostering a culture of privacy within the organization is equally important. This involves promoting awareness and providing training to employees about data protection principles and best practices. By cultivating a privacy-conscious mindset, organizations can ensure that data protection is embedded into all aspects of their operations, enhancing overall data security and compliance.

Engaging with stakeholders, including customers, employees, and regulators, is another critical practice. Regular communication and feedback with these groups help organizations understand their concerns and expectations regarding data privacy. This proactive engagement enables organizations to address issues promptly and effectively, thereby maintaining trust and demonstrating a commitment to responsible data practices.

The Impact of Data Breaches on Legal and Ethical Responsibilities

Understanding the impact of data breaches is crucial for comprehending the full scope of legal and ethical considerations in data collection and usage. This section explores how data breaches affect legal obligations and ethical responsibilities, providing insights into the ramifications for organizations and individuals alike.

Key Legal Implications of Data Breaches

Regulatory Penalties: Many jurisdictions impose fines and sanctions on organizations that fail to protect personal data adequately. These penalties can be substantial, reflecting the severity of the breach and the level of negligence involved.

Legal Actions: Affected individuals may pursue legal action against organizations for damages resulting from a breach. This can include class-action lawsuits or individual claims for compensation due to financial loss, identity theft, or emotional distress.

Compliance Costs: Organizations may face increased costs related to compliance and remediation efforts following a breach. This includes expenses for legal consultations, notifications to affected parties, and implementing enhanced security measures.

Examples are The Equifax data breach in 2017 resulted in significant regulatory fines and legal settlements due to the exposure of sensitive personal information of millions of individuals. Also, The General Data Protection Regulation (GDPR) imposes strict requirements on data breach notifications, with substantial fines for non-compliance.

Ethical Responsibilities in Response to Data Breaches

Beyond legal obligations, organizations have ethical responsibilities to address data breaches transparently and responsibly. The manner in which an organization responds to a breach can affect public trust and its overall reputation.

Transparency: Organizations should promptly and clearly communicate the details of the breach to affected individuals. Transparency involves providing information about what data was compromised, the potential impact, and the steps being taken to address the situation.

Support and Compensation: Offering support services, such as credit monitoring and identity theft protection, can help mitigate the impact of a breach on affected individuals. Compensation for damages or losses incurred as a result of the breach is also an ethical consideration.

Preventive Measures: After a breach, organizations should review and enhance their data protection practices to prevent future incidents. This includes updating security protocols, conducting regular risk assessments, and investing in employee training.

Companies like Target and Marriott International have faced scrutiny for their handling of data breaches. Effective responses that included timely notifications and proactive measures to protect affected individuals are seen as best practices. The way organizations manage public relations following a breach can influence how they are perceived. Ethical handling of the breach involves addressing concerns openly and demonstrating a commitment to preventing future incidents.

Data breaches can have a profound long-term impact on organizational practices, significantly influencing how data protection is prioritized and managed. In response to breaches, organizations often invest in enhanced security measures and technologies to bolster their defenses. This investment may include adopting advanced encryption methods, implementing multi-factor authentication, and conducting regular security audits to identify and address vulnerabilities. The experience of a data breach frequently prompts revisions to data protection policies and procedures. Organizations update these policies to better align with best practices and regulatory requirements, ensuring that they are more robust and comprehensive in safeguarding against future incidents. This ongoing refinement of practices underscores a commitment to improving data security and reinforcing the organization's resilience against potential breaches.

These breaches can catalyze significant cultural shifts within organizations, highlighting the critical importance of data protection and fostering a privacy-centric culture among employees. Such breaches often lead to a heightened emphasis on data security, prompting organizations to integrate privacy considerations more deeply into their organizational ethos. For instance, companies that have experienced breaches typically invest in more rigorous security protocols and engage in ongoing improvements to strengthen their defenses. This proactive approach reflects a commitment to bolstering their security infrastructure and preventing future incidents. Additionally, organizations frequently revise their privacy policies and data handling procedures based on insights gained from breaches. These revisions enhance overall data protection practices, ensuring that policies are updated to reflect the best practices and regulatory requirements, ultimately contributing to a more resilient and privacy-conscious organizational culture.

Navigating the legal and ethical considerations of data collection and usage is a complex but essential task in this age. By adhering to universal principles of data protection and embracing ethical practices, organizations can protect individuals' privacy, foster trust, and contribute to a responsible digital ecosystem. As technology continues to evolve, ongoing vigilance and adaptability will be key to ensuring that data practices remain aligned with both legal requirements and ethical standards.

CHAPTER TEN

FUTURE TRENDS IN ONLINE PRIVACY AND DATA PROTECTION

In an era where data is a central asset for innovation, understanding future trends in online privacy and data protection is crucial for anticipating and addressing emerging challenges. As technology evolves rapidly, so too must our approaches to safeguarding personal information. We will examine key future trends shaping the landscape of online privacy and data protection, providing insights into technological advancements, regulatory developments, and evolving societal expectations.

The Rise of Artificial Intelligence and Privacy Implications

Artificial Intelligence (AI) is set to revolutionize various aspects of life, from enhancing user experiences to optimizing business processes. However, its rise brings significant privacy implications that need to be addressed.

AI-Driven Data Collection and Analysis: AI technologies, including machine learning algorithms and predictive analytics, enable more sophisticated data collection and analysis. These technologies can process vast amounts of data to identify patterns and make predictions. While this capability offers substantial benefits, such as personalized services and improved decision-making, it also raises concerns about how personal data is collected, used, and stored.

AI systems often operate as "black boxes," meaning their internal processes and decision-making mechanisms are not easily understandable to users. This lack of transparency makes it challenging for individuals to grasp how their data is being used, which can undermine trust in these systems. Ensuring transparency in AI-driven data practices is crucial for maintaining user confidence and accountability. Additionally, AI systems can inadvertently perpetuate biases present in the data they are trained on, leading to discriminatory outcomes that affect certain groups unfairly. Addressing these biases is essential to ensure that AI applications are used equitably and do not reinforce existing inequalities. Implementing measures to enhance transparency and mitigate bias in AI systems is vital for promoting fair and responsible data practices.

Regulatory considerations for AI systems are increasingly focusing on enhancing transparency and addressing biases. One key aspect is the implementation of explainability requirements, which may mandate that organizations provide clear, understandable explanations of how AI systems process and use personal data. This requirement aims to enhance transparency, allowing users to better comprehend the mechanisms behind AI-driven decisions and fostering greater trust in these systems. In addition, legal frameworks are likely to include mandates for bias mitigation, requiring organizations to implement measures that detect and address biases within AI algorithms. These regulations seek to ensure that AI systems operate fairly and do not perpetuate or amplify existing inequalities, promoting a more equitable use of personal data and protecting individuals from discriminatory outcomes.

AI and Privacy-Enhancing Technologies: In response to privacy concerns, researchers and developers are creating privacy-enhancing technologies (PETs) that integrate with AI systems. These technologies aim to safeguard personal data while still enabling valuable insights.

One example of a privacy-enhancing technology is federated learning, which allows AI models to be trained across decentralized devices without the need to share raw data. This approach helps preserve privacy by keeping sensitive information localized and reducing the risk of data breaches. Another example is differential privacy, a technique that adds controlled noise to datasets to obscure individual identities while still enabling valuable data analysis. By implementing differential privacy, organizations can protect personal information from being identified or misused, ensuring that privacy is maintained even when analyzing large-scale datasets. Both federated learning and differential privacy represent significant advancements in safeguarding data while still deriving useful insights from it.

The regulatory landscape for data privacy is continuously evolving, with new laws and frameworks emerging to address the growing complexity of data protection. For instance, global regulatory harmonization is in the picture. As data crosses international borders, there is a growing push for regulatory harmonization to create a unified approach to data privacy. Efforts are underway to align data protection standards across different regions, making compliance more manageable for global organizations.

Initiatives aimed at enhancing global data privacy often focus on cross-border data transfers and international cooperation. Cross-border data transfer agreements and frameworks are designed to facilitate secure and compliant transfers of data between countries with differing data protection standards. These agreements help ensure that personal information remains protected even as it moves across international boundaries. International cooperation among regulatory bodies plays a crucial role in developing consistent privacy standards and sharing best practices. By collaborating, regulatory agencies can align their approaches to data protection, promote uniform privacy practices, and address the complexities of global data management more effectively. These initiatives are essential for navigating the challenges of international data privacy and fostering a more cohesive global approach to protecting personal information.

Another evolution in data privacy regulations is enhanced consumer rights. Future regulations are likely to expand consumer rights regarding data privacy, giving individuals more control over their personal information. We can anticipate to see potential developments in the right to data portability and the right to explanation. The right to data portability allows individuals to transfer their personal data easily between different service providers, empowering them with greater control over their information and fostering competition among businesses. This right facilitates a smoother transition for users who wish to switch services while maintaining the integrity of their data. The right to explanation grants individuals the ability to understand and contest decisions made by automated systems based on their data. This right ensures that people are informed about how automated decisions are reached and can challenge or seek clarification on outcomes that affect them, thereby enhancing transparency and accountability in data-driven decision-making processes. Both of these rights are crucial for reinforcing individual control and trust in data privacy.

What new opportunities and risks do emerging technologies introduce for data privacy and protection and what proactive measures can be taken to address potential vulnerabilities. A good case study is the proliferation of IoT devices and smart technologies. These devices often collect vast amounts of personal data, raising concerns about how this data is secured and used.

One major challenge is ensuring the security of data transmitted by these devices to prevent unauthorized access and breaches. As these devices collect and transmit large volumes of personal data, they become potential targets for cyberattacks, making robust security measures essential to protect this data from being compromised. Another critical challenge is implementing privacy by design, which involves incorporating privacy considerations into the design of these devices from the outset. By addressing privacy risks early in the development process, manufacturers can mitigate potential vulnerabilities and ensure that data protection is an integral part of the device's functionality. This proactive approach helps to enhance user trust and safeguard personal information in an increasingly globalized world.

To address the challenges associated with IoT devices, adopting best practices such as strong authentication and data encryption is essential. Implementing robust authentication mechanisms helps secure access to these devices, ensuring that only authorized users can interact with them. This prevents unauthorized access and potential exploitation of device vulnerabilities. Additionally, employing data encryption is crucial for protecting personal information both in transit and at rest. Encryption safeguards data as it is transmitted between devices and stored, making it difficult for unauthorized parties to intercept or access sensitive information. By integrating these practices, organizations can enhance the security and privacy of these devices, thereby mitigating risks and building user trust in their connected technologies.

A second case study is Blockchain technology. It offers promising solutions for data integrity and transparency but also presents privacy challenges that need addressing. A significant challenge is its immutable nature, particularly regarding the implementation of data deletion requests. Unlike traditional databases where data can be modified or deleted, its records are permanent and unchangeable once added to the ledger. This immutability complicates the ability to comply with data deletion requests, such as the "right to be forgotten," where individuals may wish to have their personal information removed. The transaction privacy on public blockchains poses a hurdle, as transactions are visible and traceable, potentially exposing sensitive personal information. Ensuring that these implementations respect privacy concerns while maintaining transparency and security requires innovative approaches to data management and privacy controls.

One effective approach is the use of private or permissioned blockchains, which restrict access to sensitive information by limiting participation to a selected group of authorized entities. This controlled environment enhances data privacy by preventing unauthorized access and ensuring that only trusted parties can view or interact with the data. Also, zero-knowledge proofs offer a cryptographic method for validating transactions without disclosing the underlying data. This technique allows parties to prove the validity of a transaction while keeping the details of the transaction confidential, thereby maintaining privacy while ensuring the integrity and security of the framework. By integrating these solutions, organizations can mitigate privacy concerns associated with blockchain technology while still leveraging its benefits.

The final case study is 5G Technology. The deployment of this technology is set to revolutionize connectivity by offering faster speeds, lower latency, and increased capacity for a multitude of devices. However, the widespread adoption of these networks introduces several privacy risks that need to be addressed.

One significant challenge is the increased data collection enabled by 5G's enhanced capabilities. With the proliferation of connected devices and the expanded bandwidth, the volume of personal data gathered and transmitted is greatly amplified, raising concerns about how this data is managed and protected. The complexity and scale of this network introduce new vulnerabilities that could be exploited by cybercriminals. The expansive and interconnected nature necessitates holistic security measures to protect personal data from unauthorized access and breaches. Addressing these challenges is essential to ensure that the benefits of 5G technology do not come at the expense of data privacy and security.

To mitigate the privacy challenges associated with this technology, several strategies can be employed. Implementing enhanced security protocols and encryption methods is crucial for protecting data transmitted over the networks. This involves securing both the network infrastructure and the devices connected to it to prevent unauthorized access and breaches. Additionally, adopting data minimization practices can significantly reduce privacy risks. By limiting the collection and retention of personal data to only what is strictly necessary, organizations can minimize the potential for misuse or exposure of sensitive information.

It is also imperative to explore the advances in privacy-enhancing technologies. PETs are continually changing to address upcoming privacy challenges and enhance data protection. Encryption techniques remains a cornerstone of data protection, and advances in encryption technology will play a crucial role in safeguarding personal information. A promising development is homomorphic encryption, which allows data to be processed and analyzed while still encrypted, thereby safeguarding privacy during computation. This method enables sensitive information to remain secure even when it is being used for analysis, offering a significant advancement in protecting data from unauthorized access. Another critical trend is the development of quantum-resistant encryption methods. As quantum computing advances, it presents potential threats to current encryption techniques. Quantum-resistant encryption aims to create cryptographic algorithms that can withstand the computational power of quantum machines, ensuring that data remains secure in a future where quantum threats are a reality.

Privacy-by-design, another area, approaches focus on embedding data protection measures into the development of technologies and systems from the outset, ensuring that privacy considerations are integral to their design. One example is data minimization, which involves designing systems to collect and process only the minimum amount of data necessary for the intended purpose. This approach reduces the risk of excessive data collection and potential misuse. Another example is user-centric privacy controls, which provide users with intuitive and effective tools to manage their privacy settings and preferences. By giving individuals clear and accessible options to control their data, these controls empower users to protect their own privacy and make informed decisions about their personal information. Integrating these privacy-by-design principles helps build trust and ensures that data protection is a fundamental aspect of technological development.

Societal attitudes and cultural expectations regarding data privacy are evolving, influencing how organizations approach data protection. As awareness of data privacy issues grows, individuals are becoming more conscious of how their data is collected, used, and protected. There is a rising demand for transparency, with consumers increasingly seeking clear and accessible information about data practices and privacy policies. They want to understand how their data is collected, used, and protected, which drives organizations to provide more detailed and straightforward disclosures. Additionally, there is a growing interest in privacy advocacy, with more individuals and groups supporting organizations that prioritize strong data protection. This shift underscores a broader societal focus on safeguarding personal information and holding companies accountable for their privacy practices. As awareness and concern about data privacy continue to increase, organizations are compelled to enhance their transparency and commitment to protecting user data.

Ethical data use is also on the rise, with organizations being called upon to consider the broader impact of their data practices on society. Principles of fairness and accountability are central to ethical data practices. Ensuring fairness involves designing and implementing data practices that do not result in discriminatory or unjust outcomes. This means carefully analyzing data collection and processing methods to avoid biases that could disproportionately affect certain individuals or groups. Accountability, on the other hand, requires organizations to be responsible for their data practices and to address any negative consequences that arise from their handling of personal information. This includes being transparent about data practices, responding to privacy breaches, and taking corrective actions when necessary. By adhering to these principles, organizations can foster trust and demonstrate their commitment to ethical and responsible data management.

The Future of Data Privacy in a Connected World

The interconnected nature of the modern world presents both opportunities and challenges for data privacy. As technology continues to advance, the future of data privacy will be shaped by ongoing innovation, regulatory developments, and societal expectations.

Integrating Privacy into Emerging Technologies: Future technological advancements will require the integration of privacy considerations from the outset. This includes developing new standards and best practices for emerging technologies to ensure that privacy is maintained even as innovation progresses. Examples of applying privacy principles in emerging technologies highlight the importance of integrating data protection into innovative solutions. In the context of smart cities, designing infrastructure to prioritize data privacy and security is crucial while enhancing urban services and efficiency. This involves implementing robust data protection measures to safeguard the vast amounts of information collected from various sensors and devices throughout the city, ensuring that personal data is not misused or exposed. Similarly, wearable technologies must be designed with privacy in mind, ensuring that personal data collected by these devices is managed in ways that respect user privacy and provide individuals with control over their information. By embedding privacy considerations into the development of smart city infrastructure and wearable technologies, organizations can offer advanced services and products while maintaining a strong commitment to data protection.

Collaborative Approaches to Data Protection: Addressing the complexities of data privacy in a connected world will require collaborative efforts among stakeholders, including governments, businesses, and civil society. Effective data protection strategies often involve facilitating multi-stakeholder dialogues and building global partnerships. Multi-stakeholder dialogues bring together diverse groups, including industry leaders, policymakers, academics, and civil society, to collaboratively develop and implement comprehensive data protection strategies. These discussions help ensure that various perspectives and expertise are considered, leading to more robust and inclusive privacy solutions. Additionally, global partnerships are essential for addressing cross-border data privacy issues and promoting best practices. By collaborating internationally, countries and organizations can share knowledge, harmonize privacy standards, and tackle the complexities of data protection in a globalized digital landscape. These strategies are crucial for fostering effective and coordinated approaches to safeguarding personal information across different regions and sectors.

AI-Driven Privacy Enhancements: AI technologies have the potential to significantly enhance data privacy through the development of advanced privacy-preserving techniques and tools. By leveraging AI, organizations can implement more effective measures to protect personal information and manage privacy risks. Key innovations in data privacy driven by artificial intelligence (AI) offer significant advancements in protecting personal information. Anomaly detection is one such innovation, where AI algorithms analyze large volumes of data to identify unusual patterns or anomalies that may signal a security breach or data misuse. This proactive approach allows organizations to detect and respond to potential threats more swiftly, enhancing overall security. Another innovation is automated privacy controls, where AI systems manage privacy settings and preferences automatically. This capability enables users to easily control their data-sharing choices and ensures that their privacy preferences are consistently applied across various platforms and services. Intelligent data classification is a crucial AI-driven innovation, assisting in the classification and categorization of data based on its sensitivity and regulatory requirements. This helps organizations implement appropriate data protection measures and comply with data handling policies, ensuring that sensitive information is managed in accordance with privacy standards. These advancements collectively improve the efficiency and effectiveness of data privacy management in a rapidly evolving digital landscape.

While AI offers significant potential for enhancing privacy, it also raises important ethical considerations that must be addressed to ensure responsible use of these technologies. AI systems must respect user autonomy by providing clear and informed consent mechanisms. Users should be fully aware of how their data is being used by AI systems and have the ability to opt out if desired.

Organizations must ensure transparency in AI-driven data practices, including how AI algorithms make decisions and how data is processed. Accountability mechanisms should be established to address any negative impacts or unintended consequences of AI systems on privacy. These algorithms can perpetuate existing biases in data, leading to discriminatory outcomes. It is essential to implement measures to detect and mitigate biases in AI systems to ensure fair and equitable data practices.

AI play a role in data minimization. Data minimization, which is the principle of collecting and retaining only the data necessary for a specific purpose is a fundamental aspect of data privacy. AI can support data minimization efforts by optimizing data collection and reducing unnecessary data processing. There are strategies which can be employed for the integration of AI into data minimization.

Context-aware data collection involves AI systems analyzing the context in which data is gathered to assess its relevance and necessity. This approach helps in reducing the volume of data collected and processed, ensuring that only the most pertinent information is retained. Similarly, dynamic data anonymization enhances traditional techniques by adjusting the level of anonymity based on the data's use and sensitivity. This allows for a flexible approach to protecting personal information while still enabling useful analysis. By tailoring anonymity practices to the specific needs and context of the data, organizations can better safeguard privacy while leveraging data for valuable insights.

Looking ahead, several trends and developments are likely to shape the intersection of AI and data privacy. Some of them are:

AI-Enhanced Privacy Regulations: Future data privacy regulations may incorporate AI-specific provisions to address the unique challenges and opportunities presented by these technologies. This could include requirements for AI transparency, accountability, and ethical use.

Collaborative AI Governance: The development of collaborative frameworks for AI governance may emerge, bringing together stakeholders from various sectors to establish standards and best practices for the ethical use of AI in data privacy.

AI-Powered Privacy Tools: The continued evolution of AI is likely to lead to the creation of new privacy tools and solutions that offer enhanced protection and control over personal data, helping organizations and individuals navigate the complexities of data privacy in the digital age.

The future of online privacy and data protection is characterized by rapid technological advancements, evolving regulatory landscapes, and shifting societal expectations. As we look ahead, it is essential for organizations to stay abreast of emerging trends, adopt proactive measures, and engage with stakeholders to navigate the complex data privacy environment. By integrating privacy considerations into all aspects of technology and data management, organizations can build trust, ensure compliance, and contribute to a secure and privacy-respecting digital world.

CHAPTER ELEVEN

BUILDING A SECURE CULTURE

Building a secure culture is crucial for ensuring online privacy and data protection. The level of cyber threats and privacy breaches are increasingly common, organizations and individuals must develop a comprehensive framework that integrates robust data protection practices with a strong culture of cybersecurity. This chapter will outline strategies for creating such a framework, including building a culture of security within organizations and adopting best practices for cybersecurity. By addressing these areas, both organizations and individuals can significantly enhance their defenses against data breaches and cyberattacks.

Developing a Framework for Online Privacy and Data Protection

Creating an effective framework for online privacy and data protection involves several key components, each contributing to the overall security posture of an organization or individual. This framework must address legal compliance, data governance, risk management, and continuous improvement to ensure comprehensive protection of personal and sensitive information.

Legal and Regulatory Compliance: Adhering to legal and regulatory requirements is foundational for any data protection framework. Organizations must be aware of and comply with relevant privacy laws and regulations that apply to their operations. This includes understanding jurisdictional requirements. Organizations operating in multiple regions must be familiar with the data protection laws applicable in each jurisdiction. For example, the General Data Protection Regulation (GDPR) in the European Union and the California Consumer Privacy Act (CCPA) in the United States impose specific requirements on data handling and protection.

It is also essential to conduct regular audits to ensure compliance with these regulations and helps to identify potential gaps and areas for improvement. These audits should evaluate data handling practices, consent mechanisms, and data subject rights. Finally, maintaining thorough documentation of data protection practices, policies, and procedures is essential. This documentation should be readily available for regulatory reviews and audits.

Data Governance and Management: Effective data governance and management are critical for safeguarding sensitive information and ensuring that data protection policies are consistently applied. Key aspects include data classification, access controls and data lifecycle management.

Classifying data based on its sensitivity and value helps in implementing appropriate protection measures. Organizations should categorize data into different levels, such as public, internal, confidential, and restricted, to apply specific security controls accordingly. Implementing strict access controls ensures that only authorized individuals can access sensitive data. This includes role-based access controls (RBAC), least privilege principles, and multi-factor authentication (MFA) to secure data access. Managing data throughout its lifecycle from collection and processing to storage and deletion is essential for minimizing risks. Organizations should establish policies for data retention, secure disposal, and archiving to protect data at every stage.

Risk Management: Risk management involves identifying, assessing, and mitigating potential threats to data security. Effective risk management tactics encompass risk assessments, mitigation strategies and incident response planning. Regularly conducting risk assessments to identify vulnerabilities and potential threats to data protection. This includes evaluating both internal and external risks, such as cyberattacks, data breaches, and human error.

Developing and implementing strategies to mitigate identified risks is important. This may involve deploying security technologies, improving data handling practices, and enhancing employee training. Creating a strong incident response plan to address data breaches and security incidents swiftly and effectively is paramount. The plan should outline procedures for detecting, responding to, and recovering from incidents, including communication protocols and legal obligations.

Continuous Improvement: Data protection is an ongoing process that requires continuous improvement and adaptation. Keeping up to date with the latest developments in data protection regulations, emerging threats, and technological advancements is a vital strategy. This includes participating in industry forums, attending conferences, and subscribing to relevant publications.

Regularly reviewing and updating data protection policies and procedures is essential for maintaining effective data security. This process ensures that policies remain aligned with changing regulations, technological advancements, and changes within the organization. By keeping policies current, organizations can adapt to new compliance requirements and integrate improvements that address emerging threats and opportunities. Additionally, establishing feedback mechanisms is crucial for continuous improvement. These mechanisms, which include channels for input from employees, customers, and partners, help organizations identify areas for enhancement and address any concerns that may arise. Gathering and responding to feedback allows organizations to refine their data protection practices and reinforce their commitment to safeguarding personal information, ultimately fostering a more secure and responsive environment.

Building a Culture of Cybersecurity

Building a strong culture of cybersecurity within an organization is essential for protecting data and mitigating risks. A security-conscious culture promotes awareness, accountability, and proactive behavior among employees, leading to a more resilient organization. Here are several measures you can employ to achieve this:

Leadership and Commitment: Leadership plays a critical role in establishing and promoting a culture of cybersecurity. Effective strategies include executive sponsorship, clear visions and goals and regular communication. Securing support from top executives to prioritize these initiatives and allocate resources will aid in achieving this objective. Executives should actively champion security efforts and integrate them into the organization's strategic goals.

Articulating a clear vision and setting specific goals is fundamental for aligning security efforts with overall business objectives. A well-defined vision helps ensure that all the initiatives are strategically focused and that every team member understands their role in maintaining security. This clarity fosters a unified approach to protecting the organization's data and assets. Additionally, maintaining open lines of communication about policies, updates, and incidents is crucial. Regularly sharing information keeps cybersecurity top-of-mind for employees and reinforces the importance of adhering to best practices. By consistently communicating updates and fostering transparency, organizations can ensure that employees are informed, engaged, and committed to upholding robust security measures.

Employee Training and Awareness: Training and awareness programs are vital for fostering a security-conscious culture. Key elements of an effective cybersecurity awareness program include comprehensive training and phishing simulations. Comprehensive training involves regularly providing detailed instruction on security, best practices, data protection policies, and threat awareness. This training should be tailored to the specific roles and responsibilities within the organization to ensure that each employee understands the relevant security protocols and procedures. Phishing simulations are another critical component, as they offer practical experience in recognizing and responding to potential threats. By conducting these simulations and other security awareness exercises, employees can better identify phishing attempts and other malicious activities, reinforcing the training concepts and enhancing their ability to handle real-world threats effectively. Offering continuous education and resources to keep employees informed about emerging threats, new technologies, and evolving best practices is also another method of training and awareness.

Accountability and Enforcement: Establishing clear accountability and enforcement mechanisms is crucial for maintaining a culture of cybersecurity. This includes clearly defining roles and responsibilities related to the security structure, including who is responsible for implementing and overseeing security measures.

Another means is establishing performance metrics to measure the effectiveness of these initiatives and employee adherence to policies. Metrics can help identify areas for improvement and track progress. Implementing disciplinary actions for non-compliance with laid-down policies can also be employed. This helps ensure that employees understand the importance of adhering to security practices and the consequences of failing to do so.

Promoting a Security Mindset: Fostering a security mindset involves embedding cybersecurity considerations into everyday activities and decision-making. For instance, incorporating these considerations into business processes and project planning will aid in promoting this consciousness. This ensures that security is considered from the outset and integrated into all aspects of the organization. Creating a culture where employees feel comfortable reporting security concerns, suspicious activities, and potential vulnerabilities is essential for maintaining a secure environment. Encouraging prompt reporting helps address issues before they escalate, enabling quicker resolution and reducing potential risks. Additionally, recognizing and rewarding employees who demonstrate strong security practices and contribute positively to the organization's security efforts is crucial. Positive reinforcement through recognition and rewards motivates employees and reinforces desired behaviors, fostering a proactive approach to maintaining a secure and vigilant workplace.

Best Practices for Cybersecurity

Adopting best practices for cybersecurity is essential for protecting data and maintaining a secure environment. These practices encompass various aspects including technical controls, policies, and user behavior.

Technical Controls: Implementing technical controls is a key component of a comprehensive security strategy. Best practices for maintaining robust security include ensuring that all software, including operating systems, applications, and security tools, is kept up to date with the latest patches and updates. Regular software updates are crucial as they address vulnerabilities and protect against known threats, reducing the risk of exploitation. Deploying firewalls and antivirus software is essential for defending against malicious attacks and unauthorized access. These tools must be properly configured and regularly updated to maintain their effectiveness, ensuring they can effectively block threats and safeguard the organization's digital assets. Encrypting sensitive data both in transit and at rest to protect it from unauthorized access is also a measure to take. Encryption ensures that data remains secure even if it is intercepted or accessed by unauthorized parties.

Access Management: Effective access management practices help ensure that only authorized individuals can access sensitive information. Implementing Role-Based Access Control (RBAC) and Multi-Factor Authentication (MFA) are essential practices for enhancing security. RBAC involves assigning permissions based on user roles and responsibilities, adhering to the principle of least privilege, which ensures that individuals have access only to the data and systems necessary for their specific roles. This minimizes the risk of unauthorized access and data breaches. Additionally, employing MFA enhances authentication security by requiring multiple forms of verification beyond just passwords. This additional layer of protection significantly reduces the risk of unauthorized access, as it ensures that even if one credential is compromised, additional verification steps are needed to gain access. Also conduct regular reviews of user access permissions to ensure that access levels are appropriate and that inactive or unnecessary accounts are promptly deactivated.

Incident Response and Recovery: Preparing for and responding to incidents is essential for minimizing damage and ensuring continuity. Developing and maintaining a detailed incident response plan is crucial for effectively managing security incidents. This plan should outline procedures for detecting, responding to, and recovering from incidents, including clearly defined roles and responsibilities, communication protocols, and steps for mitigating and analyzing issues. Regularly conducting incident response drills and simulations is equally important. These exercises test the effectiveness of the response plan and provide valuable training for employees on handling incidents. Drills help ensure that the organization is prepared to respond swiftly and effectively, while also identifying areas for improvement to strengthen overall incident management capabilities. Performing a thorough analysis of incidents after they occur to understand their root causes, impact, and effectiveness of the response is a core component. Lessons learned from these analyses should inform updates to the incident response plan and security practices.

User Awareness and Behavior: Promoting secure user behavior is crucial for reducing the risk of cyber threats. Best practices for maintaining robust security include implementing and enforcing strong password policies, which require complexity, length, and regular changes. Such policies help prevent unauthorized access by ensuring that passwords are difficult to guess or crack. Encouraging the use of password managers can aid users in managing and creating secure passwords, reducing the risk of password-related breaches. Secure communication practices are also essential. Educating users on the importance of avoiding the sharing of sensitive information via unencrypted channels and promoting the use of secure email and messaging platforms can help protect data from interception and unauthorized access, ensuring that sensitive information remains confidential and secure. Running ongoing awareness campaigns to reinforce key cybersecurity concepts and best practices can be employed. Regular communication helps keep security top-of-mind and reinforces the importance of adhering to policies.

Building a secure culture and framework for online privacy and data protection is an ongoing and multifaceted process. Organizations and individuals must commit to integrating robust data protection measures, fostering a culture of cybersecurity, and adopting best practices to safeguard personal and sensitive information. By addressing legal and regulatory compliance, data governance, risk management, and continuous improvement, organizations can create a strong foundation for data protection. Simultaneously, cultivating a culture of security through leadership, training, accountability, and promoting a security mindset ensures that everyone within the organization contributes to a secure environment. Adopting technical controls, effective access management, incident response strategies, and promoting secure user behavior further enhances the organization's ability to protect against cyber threats. Together, these efforts create a resilient and secure framework that upholds online privacy and data protection for their environments and tailored to their specific needs.

CONCLUSION

As we conclude our exploration of online privacy and data protection, it's crucial to reflect on the multifaceted nature of these topics and the overarching themes that weave them together. From understanding the anatomy of cyberattacks to envisioning the future of data protection, our journey has illuminated the complex landscape of safeguarding information in an increasingly digital world.

Reflecting on Key Insights

Throughout this book, we have dissected the mechanics of cyberattacks, revealing how privacy breaches occur, and the methods employed by attackers to exploit vulnerabilities. By delving into the details of encryption, we have seen how securing data in transit and at rest is paramount in protecting sensitive information from prying eyes. Our discussions on personal firewalls and antivirus software highlighted the importance of these tools in defending against malicious threats, while our examination of social engineering and phishing underscored the necessity of vigilance and informed skepticism in recognizing and resisting deceptive tactics.

We also explored the impact of big data, emphasizing the delicate balance between leveraging innovation and respecting privacy. Navigating privacy settings has become a critical skill for users, empowering individuals to secure their online accounts and control their digital footprints. The rise of the Internet of Things (IoT) introduced new risks and safeguards, prompting a re-evaluation of how connected devices are managed and protected.

Our investigation into legal and ethical considerations provided a foundation for understanding the regulatory landscape and the ethical responsibilities of organizations handling personal data. Looking ahead, future trends in privacy and data protection promise both challenges and opportunities, from advancements in technology to evolving regulatory frameworks.

Connecting the Dots

As we tie these diverse elements together, it's evident that effective data protection is not merely about adopting individual measures but about integrating them into a cohesive strategy. Building a secure and privacy-conscious environment requires a holistic approach that encompasses technical, organizational, and cultural dimensions.

<u>Technical Measures</u>: From encryption and secure communication to firewalls and antivirus software, the technical measures discussed are fundamental to protecting data. However, technology alone cannot address all privacy concerns. It's essential to continuously update and enhance these tools to keep pace with emerging threats and vulnerabilities. Investing in

cutting-edge technologies and staying informed about the latest advancements are crucial for maintaining robust defenses.

Organizational Practices: Building a culture of cybersecurity within organizations is pivotal. This involves more than just implementing policies and procedures; it requires fostering an environment where security is a shared responsibility. Regular training, clear communication, and a proactive stance on incident response help create a culture where every member of the organization understands their role in protecting data. Encouraging reporting, recognizing good practices, and maintaining transparency are all part of cultivating a security-conscious mindset.

Personal Responsibility: On an individual level, personal responsibility plays a significant role in safeguarding privacy. Understanding and managing privacy settings, using strong passwords, and being vigilant against phishing and social engineering attacks are practices that contribute to overall security. Individuals must remain informed about potential risks and adopt best practices to protect their personal data.

Ethical and Legal Considerations: Navigating the legal and ethical landscape of data protection involves understanding and complying with relevant regulations while upholding ethical standards. Organizations must ensure that their data collection and usage practices are transparent, fair, and respectful of individuals' rights. By addressing legal obligations and ethical responsibilities, organizations can build trust and demonstrate their commitment to protecting personal information.

Future Outlook

Looking forward, the future of privacy and data protection will be shaped by emerging technologies, evolving regulations, and shifting societal expectations. Innovations such as artificial intelligence, blockchain, and advancements in encryption will continue to transform the landscape, offering new tools and solutions for protecting data. At the same time, challenges such as balancing innovation with privacy, managing cross-border data transfers, and addressing the implications of new technologies will require ongoing adaptation and vigilance.

In conclusion, navigating the intricacies of online privacy and data protection is an ongoing journey. The knowledge and strategies discussed throughout this book provide a strong foundation, but the landscape is ever-changing. Staying informed, adapting to new developments, and remaining vigilant are essential for successfully protecting privacy and securing data.

As we move forward, let us embrace the journey with a commitment to continuous learning and improvement. By integrating technical measures, fostering a culture of cybersecurity, and upholding ethical standards, we can collectively work towards a safer and more secure digital world. The principles and practices explored in this book are not just theoretical concepts but actionable steps that, when implemented, can make a tangible difference in protecting our personal and organizational data.

Thank you for joining me on this exploration of online privacy and data protection. May this knowledge empower you to navigate the digital world with confidence and resilience, safeguarding the privacy and security of your data in every aspect of your online presence.

www.ingramcontent.com/pod-product-compliance
Lightning Source LLC
LaVergne TN
LVHW050149060326
832904LV00003B/81